D0394028

6 25

~~~

Elite Images and Foreign Policy Outcomes

A Study of Norway

*A Publication of the Mershon Center
for Education in National Security*

Elite Images

and Foreign Policy Outcomes

A Study of Norway

PHILIP M. BURGESS

The Ohio State University Press

UNIVERSITY OF VICTORIA
LIBRARY
Victoria, B. C.

COPYRIGHT © BY THE OHIO STATE UNIVERSITY PRESS
ALL RIGHTS RESERVED
LIBRARY OF CONGRESS CATALOGUE CARD NUMBER 67–24453

Dedicated to Rene N. Ballard
Philip S. Haring
John A. Houston
Charles O. Lerche, Jr.

who served so well for political science at Knox College

Foreword

The Mershon Center for Education in National Security represents one of the Ohio State University's commitments to policy analysis and scholarly research on the gravest global problems of our time. The Center's conception of "national security" recognizes the existence of many national securities and postulates no overriding, all-embracing definition. Not only does each nation have its image of what constitutes security, but subgroups (including various "elites" and "publics") within each nation have competing formulations of security objectives. The Mershon Center devotes a substantial share of its resources to learning more about the processes by which decisions concerning national security are reached. These processes include the mechanisms by which contending images of security are formulated and the procedures through which decision-makers choose from arrays of alternative security goals and alternative programs of action to achieve the selected goals.

In many countries at different times, the effectiveness of the policy-making process is itself an issue of public policy. The Center's continuing interest in policy-making processes is not description of the processes but discovery of the ways in which variations in the processes relate to variations in the content or substance of policy, i.e., in the outcomes of the processes of decision.

Philip M. Burgess, Assistant Professor of Political Science and Director of the Behavioral Sciences Laboratory, is one of several participants in Mershon's continuing efforts to unravel the elusive relations between process and outcome. In this book, he investigates the images that Norwegian foreign ministers and other elite decision-makers hold of their nation's interests and objectives. Professor Burgess is not content with a historical résumé of one nation's elite images of security; he extends his analysis to theorizing about the ways in which these images affect the outcomes of foreign and defense processes. Through research such as is reported in this volume, the Mershon Center hopes to demonstrate that studies of policy-making processes are not only of aesthetic interest to academic observers of politics but also that the processes are important factors in shaping the values and outcomes that are at the core of political decisions in any country at any time. As policy scientists learn more about the ways in which process shapes outcomes, decision-makers and their constituents will be better able to realize national and international security consistent with their images of preferred outcomes.

JAMES A. ROBINSON, DIRECTOR

Mershon Center
for Education in National Security

Preface

This book on Norwegian foreign policy–making focuses on the period 1940 to 1949. During this period a fundamental change occurred in Norway's foreign policy—a change from neutrality and withdrawal from international politics to active participation in the Atlantic Alliance Treaty. For Norway's experiences, like most other nations', during and after World War II had a profound impact on outlook on international politics. And the change in outlook—or rather the perception of Norway's relations in a larger international system—is a primary concern of Professor Burgess. He has largely confined his study to the perceptions of the "authoritative" elite, i.e., prime ministers, foreign ministers, and defense ministers.

When World War II broke out, Norway had enjoyed peace for 125 years—since 1814. This long span of peace was due to not only domestic forces; to a large extent it was the result of external circumstances. With her long and ice-free coast bordering the North Atlantic Ocean, Norway held an important strategic position, particularly significant for her powerful neighbor Great Britain. If some hostile great power should seize control of the Norwegian coast, this would mean a serious disadvantage for British sea power. As long as Britain was strong enough to prevent other great powers from gaining a foothold on Norwegian territory, Norway's wish to remain neutral did not conflict with British interests.

In this respect the geostrategical situation of Norway was similar to that of other nations bordering the Atlantic Ocean, the outstanding case in point being the United States of America. Protected by British sea power, these countries could develop their democratic institutions and national resources relatively undisturbed by international conflicts.[1]

This external background of Norwegian foreign politics was clearly recognized by Prime Minister Gunnar Knudsen who stated in 1914, "We trust in England." Although his statement was strongly attacked by political opponents, it is not quite clear whether this reaction was due to the bluntness of his declaration, or whether some leaders simply did not recognize the significance of strategical factors.

Neutrality and withdrawal from international conflicts were the key words of Norwegian foreign politics until World War II. After World War I Norway was an ardent supporter of the League of Nations. Pacifist sentiments were prevalent among a large proportion of the population, and national defense was reduced to a minimum. During the 1930's the defense was not improved significantly, despite growing international tension, and despite the failure of the League to maintain peace.

Both militarily and politically the German attack on Norway in April, 1940, came as a surprise. Despite rumors of an imminent German invasion, the government did not make military preparations. A leading Norwegian commentator on foreign politics at that time has told an anecdote which clearly characterizes the confusion of the situation. On April 9, when German forces invaded Oslo, and he was seeking shelter from the bombing, people came up to him and asked his expert opinion on what was happening. They wanted to know from where did the attacking airplanes come. His answer was: "They must be British, because the German Luftwaffe would not have been able to break through the British blockade of Skagerak and Kattegat." This perception of the military situation, held by an influential expert, would certainly not be expressed in public statements by the authoritative elite. Although a number of political and military leaders might not share the opinions of this commentator, his view apparently constituted an underlying strategical assumption of Norwegian foreign policy. The German attack revealed that modern warfare—in particular the development of long ranged air forces—had changed dramatically the strategical position of Norway: the country was no longer sheltered by the British navy.

The experience of the German attack and subsequent occupation led to a rethinking on Norwegian foreign politics. The discussions which were carried out in circles around the exile government in London have been extensively covered in the present volume. The government eventually arrived at the position that Norway in the future would have to solve her problem of national security in collaboration with the Western powers.

From the very beginning Norway strongly supported the collective security system of the United Nations. However, as the cold war emerged and as it was realized that the United Nations did not give sufficient security, Norwegian policy-makers were again faced with a national security problem. Three alternative solutions seemed open:

(1) the country could join Sweden and Denmark in a Scandinavian defense alliance;

(2) she could join the Western powers in the broader defense alliance that was being planned; or

(3) she could return to her prewar position of neutrality.

The last solution was never seriously considered, so the discussion focused upon the two other alternatives. The Scandinavian defense negotiations did not turn out to be successful. Although the period covered in this study ranges from 1940 to 1949, the emphasis is placed upon the period between January, 1948, when the Scandinavian negotiations started, until April, 1949, when Norway joined the Atlantic Alliance.

Indeed, the images of the authoritative elite changed during the decade of the forties. Before the war the leaders expressed the perception that great powers were immoral and undependable in their relations with other nations. From this they drew the conclusion that the safest policy for a small country was to avoid involvement in international conflicts. After the war co-operation with great powers was seen as instrumental for preserving national security. The Foreign Minister, on several occasions, expressed the view that, by being actively involved, small nations could contribute to maintaining international peace and stability.

However, in his study of foreign policy–making, Professor Burgess does not limit himself to the analysis of changing elite images. His main concern is the problem of how policy outcomes are related to leadership images. A strategical image contributes to defining the political situation for the decision-makers. When the image is given, the decision-makers are faced with the question: which alternative courses of action should be considered? Indeed, the number of alternatives as seen by the leaders is in most cases surprisingly low.

To my knowledge, this is the best study made of Norwegian foreign politics in the period since 1940. The author describes some major events in Norwegian domestic and foreign politics, a technique that aids the reader in comprehending the general context in which foreign policy decisions were made. Although he is a foreigner to the system, Professor Burgess seems to have acquired good insight in Norwegian politics. The author's interpretation is compelling (albeit pre-operational).

The author has defined the limits of his analysis as embracing largely the authoritative elite, and this limitation in focus should be kept in mind by the reader. Both before and after the war a large majority of the parliament supported the foreign policy of the government. Therefore, we may assume that the images held by the authoritative leaders would be shared by a substantial proportion of the total political elite. However, this does not mean that we should expect to find anything close to a consensus. Throughout the period the policies described have been opposed by a small, but vigorous, minority. And people who oppose the official policies are most likely to perceive international politics in a different way than authoritative leaders. Of course, we may also expect some disagreements concerning strategical images among people who otherwise tend to agree with the main conclusions of the official policies. Professor Burgess is certainly aware of this. He has extended the present work into a new study in which a number of political, administrative, and military leaders have been interviewed. In addition to giving a picture of elite image that shows subtleties and nuances, this new study is likely to produce valuable knowledge about the processes of policy-making.

In my opinion the most interesting aspect of the present volume pertains to the unsuccessful Scandinavian defense negotiations. In this analysis the author is concerned not only with Norwegian elite images; he also tries to depict strategical images of Swedish and Danish authoritative leaders. Because of differences in geostrategical position and in past experiences, the strategical images differ in several respects. For several decades efforts have been made to establish co-operation between the Scandinavian countries, culturally, economically, and politically. Although the results of these efforts have been substantial, one is left with the impression that they could have been even greater. The analysis presented here suggests that differences in elite images constitute—at least in some areas—an obstacle to Scandinavian co-operation.

The study is a good example of how elite images can contribute to explaining conflicts and co-operation among nations. In recent years we have seen a number of studies of elite images. As two outstanding examples should be mentioned Singer's study of American and Soviet elites [2] and Holsti's study on the outbreak of World War I. [3] Most of this work has focused upon the relationships among great powers. However, throughout history a great number of international conflicts have originated as controversies among small nations or as a result of their relations with more powerful neighbors. It therefore seems highly justified to focus attention—as Professor Burgess has done—upon small nations.

The methods applied may be less elaborate in the present work than in several other studies of elite images. However, the author has added a new dimension to this type of study by focusing upon the relationship between elite images and policy decisions. This book not only contributes to exploring Norwegian foreign politics, it is also a contribution of a more general character to the study of foreign policy–making.

HENRY VALEN

Department of Political Science
University of Oslo

1. For a stimulating discussion of the role of naval powers in international politics, see Alfred T. Mahan, *The Influence of Seapower upon History* (New York: Hill & Wang, 1957); first published in 1890.

2. J. David Singer, "Soviet and American Foreign Policy Attitudes: Content Analysis of Elite Articulations," *Journal of Conflict Resolution,* VIII (December, 1964), 482–85.

3. Ole R. Holsti, "The 1914 Case," *American Political Science Review,* LIX, No. 2, 365–78. For a provocative discussion of images see Kenneth E. Boulding, *The Image* (Ann Arbor: University of Michigan Press, 1956); and Kenneth E. Boulding, "National Images and International Systems," in James N. Rosenau (*ed.*), *International Politics and Foreign Policy* (New York: Free Press, 1961), pp. 391–98.

Acknowledgments

Social scientists who venture outside their own countries for purposes of research incur many debts. I am no exception. Without the benefit of the Fulbright program this study could not have been undertaken, and without the sympathetic understanding of the United States Educational Foundation in Norway, which extended the grant period from nine to twelve months, the study would not have been completed. Finally, a post-doctoral fellowship at the Mershon Center for Education in National Security at the Ohio State University permitted me the time and resources necessary to revise my original study and offer it in its present form.

Those in Norway who contributed to this study are too numerous to be named. However, an acknowledgment of gratitude must be extended to the Norwegian Institute of International Affairs, its Director, Dr. John Sanness, and Associates of the Institute, Arne Olav Brundtland and Per Frydenberg, who provided office space, tools of the trade, a pleasant atmosphere, and lively criticism. Also of great assistance in Scandinavia were Jahn Otto Johansen, then with the Oslo *Morgenposten* and now Foreign Editor of Norwegian Broadcasting, Nils Ørvik at the University of Oslo, and Nils Andrén of the University of Stockholm. In addition, I profited immeasurably from a weekly seminar with visiting and permanent research staff members at the Institute of Social Research in Oslo, especially seminar leader J. David Singer, and Henry Valen, Johan Galtung, and Mari Holmboe Ruge. I also benefited from numerous indulgences of operating policy-makers in the Foreign Office and from discussions with the many knowledgeable people who attended the various functions sponsored by the Norwegian Institute of International Affairs.

These people have all prevented many errors of judgment and fact from being included in that which follows.

A word of appreciation must also be extended to the library staffs at the Nobel Institute and the Foreign Office, who performed many thankless tasks with dispatch and thoroughness, as well as to Mr. Kjell Frank of the Storting's Library and to Diana Vidnes of the Conservative Party's Press Archives, both of whom provided the author with many valuable leads and relieved him from much of the drudgery of scholarship.

A special note of appreciation must be acknowledged to Professor H. P. Krosby of the University of Wisconsin, who provided a page-by-page critique of an early draft, and to three late friends and colleagues of the author: Mr. Helge Groth, of the Norwegian Foreign Service, who was an invaluable critic in the final stages of this project; Professor Edgar S. Furniss, Director of the Mershon Social Science Program, who encouraged the revision of the original draft and who first suggested publication; and Dr. Charles O. Lerche, Jr., who first suggested Norway as a research site and who provided guidance on an early draft, serving as chairman of my dissertation committee at the American University's School of International Service in Washington, D.C.

The author is grateful to *Foreign Affairs* for permission to quote from Halvdan Koht's "Neutrality and Peace: The View of a Small Power" in the January, 1937, issue.

Finally, I would like to express my appreciation to my wife, who performed beyond the call of duty, learning a new language, checking bibliography, typing drafts, infusing relevant criticism, and insuring (with coercion now and then) good working conditions; and to Mrs. Vicky Lankamer and Misses Donna Copen, Sandra Lindemood, and Karin Lissakers for typing and editing the manuscript. As usual, however, the author accepts responsibility for errors of omission and commission in that which follows.

P. M. B.

Columbus, Ohio
May, 1967

Contents

Elite Images and Foreign Policy Outcomes

A Study of Norway

Introduction

Foreign policy analysis.—Foreign policy case studies, single-country texts, texts on comparative foreign policy, and monographs on foreign policy analysis have been largely dominated by an "input-output" mode of analysis (although only a few of the authors would use those terms).[1] The emphasis in most studies of foreign policy are on the "factors" that "determine," or the "elements" in foreign policy–making. These usually include the "quantifiable" factors such as military capability, industrial capacity, and manpower and the "soft" factors such as national morale, diplomatic skill, and technical competence of the population. Many of the studies then describe the foreign policy objectives, interests, and outcomes of a specific country either with reference to other nations in the system or with reference to selected issues. Only occasionally are the policy outcomes linked in some way to the factors that have been selected *a priori* as relevant variables in the determination of foreign policy outcomes.

Two recent (i.e., postwar) developments have modified the emphasis in foreign policy research. First, the emergence of "peace research" resulted in the execution of research on foreign policy by psychologists, sociologists, psychoanalysts, anthropologists, and economists, each of whom brought his unique skills and points of view to his research on problems of foreign policy and international politics, skills and points of view that were alien to many of the political scientists, historians, and lawyers who had previously dominated the field.[2] Second, the advent of the decision-making approach to the study of foreign policy raised a whole series of "process" questions that seldom had been asked by previous researchers.[3] Although the work of peace researchers and the decision-making analysts have very little in common, there is a convergence of interests in their research on the role of social-psychological factors in the foreign policy matrix.[4] However, the peace research orientation tends to examine mass attitudes and focus on problems of irrationality, hostility, and other Freudian and neo-Freudian variables that fit in "the problem of human conflict" framework.[5] The decision-making analysts, on the other hand, have not given much of their time to the study of the "definition of the situation" as one of the important variables in the decision-making framework.[6] Rather, decision-making analysis has tended to emphasize process problems within and between organized decisional units, on recruitment, and on the role of planning and budgeting in policy-making. Consequently, the images of "men at the top" have been largely ignored by both groups of researchers who are most familiar with the place of psychological variables in foreign policy-making.[7]

It is hoped that this study will make a small contribution to the study of elite images and the relation of elite images to foreign policy choice situations. For the purpose of probing the relationship between elite images and foreign policy outcomes, Norway was selected as a case study. The analysis is limited to a critical nine-year period of Norwegian foreign policy, from April, 1940 (the German invasion of Norway), to April, 1949 (Norwegian accession to the Atlantic Pact), during which time cardinal foreign policy decisions were made by the Norwegian government.[8]

The strategic image as an analytical concept.—The concept *strategic image* will be used in this study to refer to the organized representation of the important features of the foreign policy environment as articulated by the authoritative decision-makers on foreign policy issues in Norway during the period under investigation. The attempt is made to reconstruct the strategic images of the two Norwegian foreign ministers during the period selected by an analysis of their public statements of policy, followed by an attempt to link the strategic image with subsequent policy choices. The descriptive portions of this study, then, are aimed at reconstructing in context the strategic image, and the thrust of analysis is to test the correspondence of policy choices to the reconstructed image. Thus, the strategic image is viewed as the independent variable of the analysis, although attention is given in passing to the process by which the image is acquired, reinforced, or modified.

Data sources and problems.—The data for the study were drawn from major statements of Norwegian foreign ministers during the nine-year period. A "major statement" is defined as a statement to the parliament (Storting) or a "major" speech as defined by, and reflected in, the press. In addition, some major statements of other relevant actors (defense ministers, prime ministers, and monarchs) are occasionally used, and reference is made during World War II to a working paper circulated in the Norwegian Foreign Office in London. Only those portions of public statements revealing of the characteristics of the components of the strategic image are used; thus many major speeches, especially during World War II, do not supply data relevant to this inquiry.

Two genuine problems of validity are encountered in a study of this kind. First, it must be asked if images studied are those of the authoritative decision-makers. In other words, if it is argued that behavioral responses to the environment are predicated on the subjective evaluation and appraisal of the environment (the image), then for the proposes of foreign policy analysis it does make a difference whose images are studied. Because it would require a study longer than that presented here to demonstrate that the *de facto* decision-makers have been selected, this aspect of the validity problem must be recognized as a limitation of this study.[8] The second aspect of the validity issue is the ubiquitous problem of confidence that an analysis of articulations is, in fact, tapping real beliefs, appraisals, and evaluations. And there is the related question regarding the sufficiency of public articulations as reliable indicators of private beliefs.[9] In an attempt to mitigate the difficulties posed by these aspects of the validity problem, all statements, including those which are somehow inconsistent with the mold of the analytical development, are presented in context and related one to another and to subsequent behavior.

The nature of a strategic image.—As used in this study, a strategic image is assumed to have two analytically distinguishable components: the cognitive and the affective. The *cognitive* component of a strategic image refers to the policy-maker's view and definition of the central features of the international environment. These characteristics of the environment constitute, from the point of view of the policy-maker, "objective reality," and are independent of his response to it. The *affective* component of a strategic image refers to the valuational dimension of the policy-maker's image structure. Here he assigns his liking or disliking, his approval or disapproval to those conditions, persons, or entities that he "knows" exist. Foreign policy actions refer to the response (or set of responses) that the policy-maker thinks is required by, or appropriate to, the environment as defined by the cognitive and affective components of the strategic image.[10]

The term *strategic image,* then, is used to summarize the way in which a policy-maker organizes, structures, evaluates, and relates to his environment. In addition, a strategic image has a *selecting* function, filtering the many bits of information that are continually emitted by the environment. Both the cognitive and affective components, for example, will "accept" information that reinforces the policy-maker's view of the environment, while they will tend to reject information that would require image modification. Although some images are probably more susceptible of modification or revision via feedback process than others, that is, some are less rigid or more "open" than others, one of the characteristics of an image is its stability over time. An image may be revised, for example, by a traumatic experience or a series of image-denying events demonstrating its lack of correspondence to reality and thereby undermining its stability. Or, in the specific case of images affecting foreign policy behavior, a change in top personnel may result in a new operational strategic image, since images are associated with individuals.[11] Whatever the image is, however, it is the image through which stimuli are filtered (not the stimuli themselves) on which behavior is predicated. In performing this function, the strategic image is a more comprehensive concept for that which has been identified as the "psychological environment."[12] A strategic image has an *integrating* function, permitting the policy-maker to "make sense" out of and thereby organize and integrate the information he daily receives. And it has an *orienting* function, clarifying expectations about the future for the policy-maker and thereby linking the cognitive and affective components with action. This permits the policy-maker to plan for contingencies and select courses of action designed to modify, deter, accommodate, or accelerate subjectively probable trends or perceived conditions. For the purposes of foreign policy analysis, the orienting function may be among the most important justifications for image analysis. Because policy-making is future-oriented, courses of action are to a large extent determined by the policy-maker's subjective calculations of future configurations and their relation to postulated goals. Viewed in this way, foreign policy might be defined as courses of action selected by decision-makers that are designed to facilitate, accommodate, modify, or prevent predicted future configurations and conditions.

The utility of image analysis.—An image is a dynamic concept; that is, images are continually subject to redefinition as a result of the operation of interactive and feedback processes. Therefore, it is somewhat artificial to view an image as either a dependent or independent variable. (In fact, it will be noted in this study that the strategic image will be presented in a series of "cross sections" permitting a description of changes that may have occurred in cognition, or affect, and thereby make the link to subsequent choices.) With this caveat in mind, however, it can be noted that most image analysis in political science and international politics treat the image as a dependent variable.[13] The modal studies with this focus are those dealing with aspects of political socialization. Related to this, it should be noted that most studies deal with the images of attentive or expressive publics and not with authoritative decision-makers. One reason for this, undoubtedly, is the increase of data made available by improved survey methods; also, analysts take added comfort in working with samples of larger, less ephemeral populations. Although a few studies do deal with images as independent variables,[14] they are, for the most part, limited to what has been identified here as the affective component of the strategic image, focusing on factors such as threat or hostility,[15] and very few of these focus on top echelon decision-makers.

In addition to the methodological problems acknowledged above, the utility of image analysis remains to be demonstrated, but systematic research might lead to some of the following payoffs. First, the reconstruction and analysis of strategic images might lead to reliable "negative prediction," that is, systematic, longitudinal analysis of the cognitive and affective components might permit foreign policy analysts to predict with confidence courses of action that will *not* be selected, alternatives that will *not* be chosen (or even considered), and options that will *not* be explored. Second, strategic images may prove to have considerable explanatory power. That which appears "irrational" to the outside observer might be quite consistent with and rational when viewed in the framework of the strategic image of the actor. In any case, the utility of image analysis for explaining foreign policy outcomes probably will not be less than that provided by analyses of capability or ideology and might prove to be a useful supplement to the more conventional concepts. Third, strategic images are especially susceptible of comparative analysis, as will be demonstrated in a portion of this study. Finally, the accumulation of *hard knowledge* by a rigorous and reliable elaboration of the strategic images of "other" national elites and aspiring elites might be a powerful policy tool. Like all knowledge, it could be used for good or ill, but accumulated systematically such knowledge would provide a good indicator of those aspects of the friend or adversary's image that require modification or reinforcement as a prerequisite to attainment of a goal, and it would aid in the anticipation of conflict, impasse, or agreement among elites over different issue areas.

There are also limitations to image analysis in addition to those of a methodological nature already acknowledged. In the absence of research, it might be suggested that the connection between a strategic image and policy outcomes might vary from country to country, from time to time, and perhaps even over different issue areas. This "hunch" is proffered because it is probable that in many cases the strategic image of authoritative decision-makers is mediated by other agencies of the decision-making process and by competing strategic images among decision-makers. Further research, however, may demonstrate that the mediation of strategic images occurs in a systematic way when associated, for example, with different issues or political systems.

Interesting and important as many of these questions are, most of them will not be examined in this study. As mentioned in the beginning, the study is an exploration. It attempts only to probe the utility of strategic-image analysis as a negative predictor and as a tool for explanation. Tentative judgments can be based on that which follows.

The first chapter of this study is devoted to placing Norwegian foreign policy in context by a brief review of societal and governmental factors followed by a survey of Norway's historical role in the international system. The following chapters attempt to show the evolution of the Norwegian strategic image and to relate the image to subsequent policy outcomes.

---

1. Cf. Kurt London, *The Making of Foreign Policy: East and West* (New York: Lippincott, 1965); Joseph E. Black and Kenneth W. Thompson (eds.), *Foreign Policies in a World of Change* (New York: Harper & Row, 1963); Roy C. Macridis (ed.), *Foreign Policy in World Politics* (Englewood Cliffs: Prentice-Hall, 1965); Martin Needler, *Understanding Foreign Policy* (New York: Holt, Rinehart & Winston, 1966); Feliks Gross, *Foreign Policy Analysis* (New York: Philosophical Library, 1954); and George Modelski, *A Theory of Foreign Policy* (New York: Praeger, 1962).

2. For an excellent example of this multidisciplinary research effort see the essays in Elton B. McNeil (ed.), *The Nature of Human Conflict* (Englewood Cliffs: Prentice-Hall, 1965). See also the lead editorial in the first issue of *Journal of Peace Research* (1964), pp. 1–4.

3. Richard C. Snyder, H. W. Bruck, and Burton Sapin, *Foreign Policy Decision Making* (New York: Free Press, 1962), *passim*.

4. Compare, for example, Snyder, *et al., op. cit.*, with essays in McNeil, *op. cit.*

5. See, for example, Otto Klineberg, *The Human Dimension in International Relations* (New York: Holt, Rinehart & Winston, 1965), *passim*.

6. See Snyder, *et al., op. cit.*, especially pp. 62 ff.; see also, Herbert A. Simon, *Administrative Behavior* (New York: Free Press, 1957), especially chap. v; James G. March and Herbert A. Simon with Harold Guetzkow, *Organizations* (New York: Wiley, 1965), especially chap. vi; Richard C. Snyder and James A. Robinson, *Nations and International Decision Making* (New York, Institute for International Order, n.d.), esp. Projects 49–54.

7. A partial exception to the point made here is the work of Ole Holsti. See his study of Dulles, "The Belief System and National Images: A Case Study," in Davis B. Bobrow (ed.), *Components of Defense Policy* (Chicago: Rand-McNally, 1965), pp. 375–89. A conceptual innovation in foreign policy analysis that should permit a meaningful linkage of these two approaches is presented by James N. Rosenau, "Pre-Theories and Theories of Foreign Policy," in R. Barry Farrell, *Approaches to Comparative and International Politics* (Evanston, Illinois: Northwestern University Press, 1966), pp. 27–92.

8. A thorough discussion of both the advantages and potential dangers of focusing on the individual decision-maker as an actor in the foreign policy process is found in Herbert Kelman, "Social-Psychological Approaches to the Study of International Relations: The Question of Relevance," in Herbert Kelman (ed.), *International Behavior* (New York: Holt, Rinehart & Winston, 1965).

9. For a discussion of these and related problems see Ithiel de Sola Pool (ed.), *Trends in Content Analysis* (Urbana: University of Illinois Press, 1959).

10. For a provocative discussion of images see Kenneth E. Boulding, *The Image* (Ann Arbor: University of Michigan Press, 1956); see also William A. Scott, "Psychological and Social Correlates of International Images," in Kelman (ed.), *op. cit.*

11. On the other hand, it might be argued that recruitment patterns and communication structures in organizations tend to perpetuate images, regardless of leadership. See Boulding, *op. cit.*, and Kenneth E. Boulding, *Conflict and Defense: A General Theory* (New York: Harper & Row, 1963), especially chap. viii.

12. Harold and Margaret Sprout, "Environmental Factors in the Study of International Politics," in James N. Rosenau (ed.), *International Politics and Foreign Policy* (New York: Free Press, 1961).

13. The first section of Kelman (ed.), *op. cit.*, deals in part with images viewed as dependent variables, whereas the second deals with images as independent or mediating variables.

14. See, for example, J. David Singer, "Soviet and American Foreign Policy Attitudes: Content Analysis of Elite Articulations," *Journal of Conflict Resolution,* VIII (December, 1964), 482–85.

15. For example, see Dina A. Zinnes, Robert C. North, and Howard E. Koch, Jr., "Capability, Threat, and the Outbreak of War," in Rosenau, *op. cit.*

CHAPTER I

Norwegian Foreign Policy
in Perspective

A country profile.—Norway, situated on the north and west littoral of the Scandinavian peninsula, is Europe's fifth largest country in land area and, after Iceland, its most sparsely populated nation. Norway is located next to the Atlantic and the North Sea on its western, northern, and southern flanks and has a coastline, punctuated by deep, ice-free fjords, of more than 17,000 miles. On its eastern flank it shares a long common frontier with Sweden and mutual borders with Finland and the Soviet Union.[1] In addition, Norway has overseas island possessions, the most important of which is her Arctic possession of Svalbard,[2] which have a total land area one-fifth the size of Norway itself.[3]

Norway's population, slightly exceeding three and one-half million, is concentrated along the coastal areas and around the deep inland fjords, with three quarters of the people living within ten miles of the sea.[4] With one exception,[5] there are no important minority groups, and all share the same Lutheran religion, yet the important sections of the country are relatively isolated as a result of two intersecting mountain ranges, a sectional isolation that is only beginning to be overcome with an improved communications system.[6] The population distribution of the country has been characterized by a movement toward the urban districts and a propensity to settle in the area around the Oslofjord.[7]

The segregation of the Scandinavian peninsula as a consequence of its historical remoteness from the main currents of European life has resulted in the phenomenon of a highly individualized ethnic composition referred to as "Nordic." The Nordic peoples are found in Norway, Sweden, Denmark, Iceland, and Finland,[8] but the least departure from the idealized type is found in Iceland, Norway, and Sweden [9] as a result of the absence of intrusion of other ethnic elements that have penetrated Denmark and Finland. In addition, the term *Nordic* also has cultural overtones in that the Nordic peoples share a common political history, revolving around the hub of either Sweden or Denmark,[10] common living conditions and welfare norms, a language affinity,[11] and they subscribe to many common viewpoints with regard to economic and political questions, both domestic and international.

With the exception of water resources, Norway is a country poorly endowed with natural resources, and less than five per cent of her total land area is fit for cultivation. Although Norway is self-sufficient in some of her agricultural requirements, her economy, the backbone of which is industry and commerce, has been marked by a steady decline in the number of people engaged in agriculture.[12] Norway remains a net commodity importer,[13] and the high living standard enjoyed by the nation depends on a substantial foreign trade.

A major factor in Norway's international trading position is her merchant fleet, which is today the fourth largest in the world.[14] Every year commodity imports greatly exceed commodity exports, and international payments are only balanced (when they are) by earnings from the shipping fleet. Norway, therefore, is very sensitive to international trade patterns, to conditions which affect international trade, and to the shipping policies of the great export nations of the world.[15] That Norwegian living standards could not be maintained without the "invisible earnings" of her merchant marine cannot be doubted, and it is in this sense that Norway is a maritime nation.[16]

In addition to the revenues earned by shipping, Norway has a large export trade in commodities, the most important of which are, in order, the products of the electrometallurgical and electrochemical industries, fish products, and lumber products. Her primary export customers are, in order, the United Kingdom, West Germany, Sweden, and the United States.

Norway's present political system is based on the Eidsvoll Constitution of 1814,[17] drawn after the four-hundred-year-old union with Denmark was dissolved in the wake of the Napoleonic wars (and before Norway was forced to accept a union with Sweden as a separate kingdom under the Swedish royal house). During the period of the union of Norway-Sweden,[18] however, the Constitution was operative and Norway thus has a long, unbroken history of constitutional stability even though it is a *de jure* sovereign state only since 1905.

Norway is a unitary state with a hereditary constitutional monarch exercising power in concert with a parliamentary supported Cabinet.[19] Legislative power is vested in the Storting, a modified unicameral parliament [20] consisting of 150 members elected for four-year terms [21] by a system of proportional representation from twenty geographically demarcated electoral districts.

Norway has a multiparty system with seven parties having secured parliamentary representation in the seven postwar elections.[22] The major socialist party is the Labor party, followed by the Socialist Peoples' party and the Communist party. The major non-socialist party is the Conservative party. The other non-socialist parties are the Center party (formerly the Agrarian party), the Christian Peoples' party, and the Liberal party. Arranged on the political spectrum from left to right, the Norwegian party system would appear thusly: socialist—Communist, Socialist Peoples', Labor; non-socialist—Liberal, Center (Agrarian), Christian Peoples', Conservative.

Although important differences in outlook, policy, and ideology exist among all Norwegian parties, the most important division in terms of the general domestic political debate is that which exists between the socialist and non-socialist parties.[23] However, even this dichotomy loses relevance when it comes to the conduct of Norwegian foreign policy, for, with the exception of the Moscow-oriented Communist party and the neutralist

Socialist Peoples' party,[24] the other Norwegian political parties are in fundamental agreement on the main lines of Norway's foreign and defense policies, i.e., participation in the Western alliance system, support for the United Nations, and experimentation in economic co-operation in Western and Northern Europe.[25] In terms of foreign policy, the more meaningful division in Norwegian political life is to be found *within* the Labor party and, since its formation in 1961, *between* the Socialist Peoples' party and the other Norwegian political parties.[26] Apart from its commitment to doctrinaire socialism in domestic affairs, the Socialist Peoples' party is committed *inter alia* to extricating Norway from NATO, unilateral disarmament, a formalized nuclear free zone in Northern Europe, and aloofness from Continental economic experiments.

With regard to the institutional arrangements affecting foreign policy, it should be noted that Norway, during the period 1935–65, had only three foreign ministers, all members of the ruling Labor party.[27] Norway has a conventional ministerial establishment with the Department of Foreign Affairs, divided into seven bureaus [28] and manned by both career civil servants and professional Foreign Service personnel numbering around two hundred,[29] playing the primary role in the planning, administration, and implementation of foreign policy.

The parliament's competence in foreign affairs (e.g., treaties and finance) is exercised ultimately in the plenary sessions but operationally through its Standing Foreign Affairs and Constitution Committee.[30]

The Foreign Affairs Committee acts as a consultative organ for the government and disposes of all the preliminary work on foreign affairs with which the parliament must eventually deal. In addition, there is the Enlarged Committee on Foreign Affairs, constituted by the membership of the Standing Committee and supplemented by the President and Vice-President of the Storting and up to nine other members. This committee is activated whenever matters of great importance in either foreign or defense policy must be decided by the government. Because of the confidential nature of the discussions in the Enlarged Committee, it normally meets in executive session. The point is, however, that the Enlarged Committee, consisting as it does of members of the opposition parties, permits the leading members of the Storting to have more detailed and intimate knowledge of, and familiarity with, the important and vital questions of Norwegian foreign and defense policy problems.[31]

As in other parliamentary systems, Norwegian foreign policy is a product as well as a responsibility of party and a prerogative of the prime minister. Norwegian foreign policy, however, has been largely shaped by strong and esteemed foreign ministers who have enjoyed wide reputation throughout the country. This has been particularly the case during the postwar period, during which time Norwegian foreign policy has been marked by a persisting "multipartisanship" and has displayed a remarkable continuity, reflecting, undoubtedly, the unparalleled continuity of leadership, both in the person of the Foreign Minister and his party.[32]

An overview of Norway in world affairs.—For more than four hundred years, from the fourteenth century until the conclusion of the Napoleonic Wars, Norway had little opportunity to assert her independence in either her domestic or foreign policy: Copenhagen was the center of Norwegian political, economic, and cultural life.[33] During the course of the Napoleonic debacle, however, Denmark became involved on the side of France as a result of a conflict with Great Britain and subsequently paid for its error in political judgment with the loss of Norway. Thus the Napoleonic Wars had their impact in Northern Europe too,[34] and while Norway gained in the long run from the imbroglio on the Continent, Sweden was the immediate benefactor of the Continental turbulence and Danish misfortune.

Sweden, under the *de facto* leadership of a former Marshal of Napoleon,[35] was given title to Norway by the Treaty of Kiel in 1814 as compensation for the loss of Finland to Russia in 1809.[36] The transfer of sovereignty as demanded by the treaty and supported by the great powers was not, however, to be easily or quickly effected.[37] The Norwegians considered themselves independent [38] and accordingly called together a constitutional convention which subsequently wrote and adopted a liberal and progressive basic law for an independent Norway.[39] A previous Swedish offer of a constitution had been rejected, and Sweden, with the diplomatic support of the great powers, crossed the Norwegian border in the summer of 1814 for the purpose of forcing Norwegian submission. After a war of less than three weeks, an armistice [40] was signed, and, in the fall,[41] the Norwegian Storting agreed to the election of the Swedish King to the Norwegian throne. Later [42] the Swedes accepted Norwegian modifications of the terms for union, and Norway was declared by the Act of Union to be a "free, independent, and indivisible kingdom, united with Sweden under one King." [43] Thus Norway succeeded in escaping the harsh terms of the Treaty of Kiel and in gaining a measure of independence (if not sovereignty) for the first time in four centuries, although she was tied to the Swedish crown and exercised no control over her external affairs.

The period of the union was not always satisfactory for either of the parties: [44] the Swedes were determined to exercise their authority over the Norwegians, while the Norwegians, looking to the Eidsvoll Constitution and the terms of the Act of Union, were determined to exploit to the maximum the freedom of action which had been secured.[45]

During the period of the union, Norwegian nationalism, expressed in language disputes, literature, and political demands, bloomed. Although the underlying issue between the two countries was status (that is, complete independence for Norway), the *cause célèbre* of the non-violent, quasi-constitutional dissolution of the union in 1905 [46] was the issue of control over foreign policy focused on the specific issue of a separate Norwegian consular service to enhance Norwegian commerical and shipping interests, which had grown rapidly during the nineteenth century, especially after the repeal of the British Navigation Acts in 1849.[47]

Two other developments worthy of note occurred during the period of the union. First, the century was an era of rising sentiment embracing "Scandinavianism." The movement, tied to the liberal forces awakening in Europe, began to assert itself in the early 1840's.[48] Although the Scandinavian movement was to founder on the rock of Bismark's "blood and iron" policies during the Schleswig-Holstein crisis,[49] it turned thought in Scandinavia to concepts and action [50] transcending mere co-operation and collaboration, nourishing proposals for a Northern customs union, political amalgamation, and a defense union among the three Scandinavian countries. After the failure of Norway-Sweden to come to the aid of Denmark in 1864, even though diverse motivations existed in the three countries favoring "Scandinavianism," and notwithstanding the fact that support for a pan-Scandinavian union was weakest in Norway, it is important to recognize that there existed in Norway even during the period of Swedish "subjugation" a latent Scandinavianism which has continued, reinforced, into the middle of the twentieth century, based on geographic propinquity, common culture, race, religion, common laws, institutions, and language, and similar political and commercial interests. As one distinguished student of the North has observed, although the attempts toward political amalgamation were unsuccessful, they left a "weighty heritage" [51] which was to surface time and again in their future relations.[52]

A second important development during the period of the union was the emergence of Norwegian liberalism and nationalism. Norwegian nationalism, partly as a result of her affiliation with a less progressive Sweden, can be viewed largely as a response to democratic ideas,[53] and it expresses a repugnance of great power politics that so often appeared to work to the disadvantage of Norway. These ideas were given perhaps their clearest expression by one of Norway's literary giants [54] who worked indefatigably for the cause of peace among nations, and who also enjoyed considerable political influence in Norway. Consequently, in 1890, the Norwegian Storting passed by a large majority a resolution supporting general arbitration treaties, becoming the first national assembly to do so.[55] In the same year, achieving another first, it sent delegates at public expense to the first Interparliamentary Conference. There emerged in Norway an undeniably pacifist national ideology which, as far as relations among nations were concerned, anticipated international law as the rule, adjudication as the means, and political non-involvement as the strategy for peace. This approach was not entirely shared by Norway's Scandinavian neighbors however. The Swedes possessed a relatively recent glorious past and deep-rooted military traditions; the Danes, tied, as it were, to the Continent were forced to learn the admonitions of balance-of-power politics; the Norwegians, however, enjoying the isolation afforded by geography and lacking either a recent glorious past or a military tradition, became the spokesmen for a new and growing movement in international relations.[56]

After Norway achieved independence from Sweden in 1905, her participation in international affairs, as would be expected in view of her political ideas and her world-wide shipping interests, was largely in the commercial arena. Norway's primary goal in the political arena was to secure a great power guarantee of her neutrality. In 1898 and again in 1902, prior to the dissolution of the union with Sweden, Norway alone attempted to obtain a great power guarantee of perpetual neutrality, but these attempts were blitzed on both occasions by the objections of Sweden.[57] During the period of the union, Norway-Sweden did succeed in obtaining a guarantee of integrity from France and the United Kingdom in the so-called November Treaty of 1855, but independence in 1905 terminated the November Treaty. Norway's search for a substitute guarantee of both her integrity and neutrality finally reached fruition in 1907 when she received a guarantee of integrity (but not neutrality) from France, Germany, and the United Kingdom.[58]

Norway's concern for neutrality has many sources. One of these is rooted in the long union with Sweden. Sweden, under the leadership of Karl Johan, determined after the Napoleonic Wars to forego both her former great power pretentions and her claims against Russia in Finland.[59] In addition to the above-mentioned November Treaty, Sweden made several neutrality declarations on behalf of both countries during the period of the union. As one student of the North has observed, the nineteenth century was the "century of success" for the neutrality policy of

Norway-Sweden; [60] thus a policy of neutrality had a pragmatic appeal to the Norwegian people.

Another source is to be found as a consequence of Norwegian shipping interests, income from which was a *sine qua non* for her continued livelihood at home. As a shipping nation, Norway was concerned with maintaining the prerequisites of wide commercial intercourse and thereby increased earnings for her merchantmen. In the event of war, on the other hand, Norway was concerned with maintaining neutrality and being recognized as such in order to enjoy the rights and privileges that neutral nations possessed in times of international conflict.

Norwegian neutrality is also rooted in the liberal and peace movement of the latter part of the nineteenth century. A strong movement with a pacifist orientation emerged in Norway, advocating international arbitration treaties and other international legal arrangements, often with the official support of the Norwegian government. Thus, the Norwegian concept of neutrality differed fundamentally from the concept of armed neutrality practiced by the Swedes: the Norwegians looked more to the international status of states like Belgium and Switzerland than to the international posture of her former overseer. [61]

Finally, during the nineteenth century the Norwegians had become, understandably, an intensely nationalistic people whose concern for sovereignty was enveloped in much emotion and linked to a profound skepticism for, and mistrust of, the great powers specifically and alliance systems generally. As one student of Norwegian foreign policy has observed,

as an independent nation Norway wished to keep far away from the politics of the large nations and anything that smacked of alliances. Instead, it based its policy on rigorous and impartial neutrality. This, in the opinion of the people and their leaders, was the best and most effective way to keep out of future conflicts between the major powers. Military preparedness . . . was allowed to lapse. International law and world opinion, not physical force, were to ensure peace and independence. [62]

In summary, Norway, after independence, adopted a posture of strict neutrality. Her immediate objective, universal recognition of her neutral status, was not achieved; therefore Norway's neutral status was based primarily on her own unilateral declaration, and it was supplemented by a policy of non-involvement in political affairs outside Scandinavia.

In the few years following the acquisition of independence by Norway, very little of a concrete nature was achieved in intra-Scandinavian co-operation. To most Norwegians "Scandinavian co-operation" was little more than a euphemism describing a coerced relationship with her neighbors to the east and south that always worked to Norway's disadvantage. Norway, after independence, assumed an international posture of non-involvement and isolation; she certainly did not rely on her Scandinavian neighbors to help her maintain her newly-won freedom.

If the Norwegians searched anywhere for protection and security, they looked west and primarily to Great Britain. The interest was mutual. The British had given diplomatic support to the Norwegian government during the union dissolution crisis of 1905. The British had a strategic interest in Norway and a concomitant fear that in the event of war Norway might be involved in the conflict on the German side because of the German orientation of Sweden, particularly the Swedish royal house. That Britain would not permit, insofar as she could shape events, German control of the strategic southern and western Norwegian coastal areas (and thereby the North Atlantic and the North Sea) was axiomatic in British policy. And this issue was especially pronounced in view of Germany's expanding naval capability.[63] Thus the British had little to gain from promoting a Scandinavianism in which the Swedes would necessarily wield great influence. Moreover, after the break with Sweden, the relationship between Norway and Great Britain was further strengthened by the election to the vacant Norwegian throne of Prince Charles of Denmark (Haakon VII), who was married to Princess Maud, the daughter of Edward VII.[64] However, the potential for a close alignment between the two countries was not to manifest itself for many decades.

It should be remembered that the mystique of Scandinavianism, which became unusually compelling around the middle of the nineteenth century in Norway, Denmark, and Sweden, always had less support in Norway than in any other of the Scandinavian countries. It is generally supported by historians that Scandinavianism has its strongest proponents in Denmark, even though (or perhaps because!) politically Denmark is required to be very sensitive and responsive to the policies of her southern and eastern neighbors. Sweden, on the other hand, was primarily a Baltic country, and enjoyed very friendly relations with, and had concrete ties to, Germany, while her relations with her eastern neighbor, Russia, have never been especially good, with both nations, at one time or another, having exercised hegemony over the other. Norway, however, was long oriented toward the Atlantic. Her relations with Germany were less than satisfactory, dating back as far as the Hanseatic period in Norway, although Norway's relations with Russia have always been proper, and her ties with England, as suggested above, have been especially close.

With the approach of World War I, the Scandinavian states began to rely on each other in order to maintain and, if possible, co-ordinate their separate neutrality policies in the event of war among the Continental powers. As early as 1907, a northern inter-parliamentary union was formed to further concerted action, to consider questions of international law, and to develop, maintain, and channel a higher level of responsiveness among the elites in Scandinavian states.[65] Thus, with the war approaching, the groundwork for co-operation, and particularly the co-ordination of foreign policies, had been laid, even though intra-Scandinavian relations were not entirely free from suspicion.[66]

In 1912, the three countries issued identic notes of neutrality, agreeing at the same time not to block the passages to the Baltic,[67] and finally in August of 1914, the three countries again declared in identic notes their neutrality, Norway and Sweden having added to their declarations a mutual pledge not to attack each other.[68] Scandinavian co-operation in the flush of war was possible since all three had similar needs, fears, and complaints. In the winter of 1914,[69] there occurred a dramatic meeting of the three monarchs of the Scandinavian states in Malmö, Sweden. The meeting was the first among the sovereigns of the three countries since 1363 when their predecessors met in Copenhagen. The meeting was called at the initiative of the Swedes, and the three kings affirmed their determination to keep out of the hostilities. Thus the Scandinavians attempted to isolate themselves from the war by a primitive form of collaboration in a policy based on the impartial, disinterested, and passive concept of neutrality, supplemented by an intra-Scandinavian "peace entente" symbolizing the unanimity of the Scandinavian peoples in upholding the policy of neutrality.[70]

Throughout the war, the monarchs, prime ministers, and foreign ministers of the three countries co-operated closely in their relationship to the on-going war. They held annual meetings, assumed common positions, issued joint statements,[71] and in the process they mitigated much of the animosity that had marred their relations over the preceding years. The experience was not without great significance, and one Norwegian has suggested that it was in World War I that the idea that Norway and Sweden should never come in conflict with each other became an operational assumption of Norwegian foreign policy.[72]

Too much, however, can be made of intra-Scandinavian co-operation during World War I. Even though co-operation was intimate in the areas of economic and security (i.e., neutrality) policy, contemporary observers noted that even this form of collaboration was not "sufficiently binding to place all Scandinavia in alignment with either of the belligerent groups in case one or the other becomes involved." [73]

Notwithstanding the fact that an articulate group of activists in Norway wanted to side with the Entente during the war, Norway, like the rest of Scandinavia, succeeded in keeping out of the conflict.[74] And notwithstanding the fact that Norway several times came very close to involvement in the conflagration—challenged by the Germans, the British, and the Americans, the lesson of World War I appeared to the Norwegian to be that his country would be able to maintain its independence and non-participation in future great power contests.

The majority of the Norwegians felt that this stood in connection with other nations' special respect for Norway as a small, peace-loving, and highly cultured nation.[75]

Another historian of the Norwegian experience in World I stated optimistically,

In her ability to remain neutral, Norway demonstrated to the world that it is possible for a nation to maintain peace with honor even under the most extreme provocation, if one has the will to do so.[76]

Others, however, have observed (with the benefit of hind-sight) that the Norwegian experience in the war was hardly a cause for hope. In a study of neutrality, the Scandinavian experience was characterized thusly:

The small neutral countries were not given much of a choice as to the maintenance of their neutrality. Squeezed, battered, and beaten from both sides, they were compelled to do what was expedient rather than what was desirable from their own point of view. . . . The Scandinavian countries were almost completely at the mercy of the Allies as far as trade was concerned.[77]

Norway's position was especially vulnerable since she could not claim self-sufficiency to the degree demonstrated by Sweden, and "her trade and commerce had for centuries been tied up with Great Britain and the Western world." [78] One observer of the period has summed up Norwegian policy in World War I as follows:

It is obvious that the neutrality Norway claimed to maintain was not a real one. Although Norway must be recognized as a non-belligerent . . . how much was left of her declared status. . . ? She was not impartial, nor was she passive; thus what remained of her neutrality? . . . Because war as an instrument of practical politics was out of the question, Norway was left with one alternative: to keep peace at the sacrifice of her full sovereign status. She had to take what she was given, and what little bargaining power she had did not prove sufficient to preserve her right of self-determination in her economic life.[79]

Nevertheless, Norway's neutral policy, regardless of the degree to which it deviated from legal norms, was successful in the pragmatic sense: it kept the country out of war, and most historians and politicians writing at the time saw no reason to doubt that it could work again in the event of future conflict.

Prior to the conclusion of World War I, the Scandinavian states, in sympathetic response to the declared intentions of the Allies, established government commissions with jointly drafted proposals for an international juridical organization, clearly revealing their bias in favor of any new form of organized international co-operation. Although the Scandinavian states were not invited formally to present their views during the formative stages of the League of Nations, it was nonetheless evident that they preferred an international arrangement providing procedures for conciliation and arbitration, and not a political organization that might pose a threat to a national policy of neutrality.[80] In addition to their substantive content, their common proposals are significant indications of the emergence of a co-ordinated foreign policy in peacetime by the Scandinavian states, making the first halting steps toward "bloc politics" in international organization.[81]

The Scandinavian states, with some caution and skepticism, accepted their invitation to join the League, becoming members in March, 1920.[82] The Scandinavians, and particularly the Norwegians, were as skeptical about the initial absence of an international court of justice and of concrete institutionalized procedures for conciliation as they were concerned about the inclusion of provisions for military and economic sanctions. The skepticism regarding great power intentions and idealism voiced by the Norwegian Labor party was echoed throughout much of Scandinavia,[83] and these doubts were often given official expression in the repeated efforts of the Scandinavian states "to transform [the League] from a political organization into an instrument for the peaceful solution of all disputes."[84] Furthermore, in view of the sanctions system embodied in Article XVI, many asserted that the Scandinavians had placed in jeopardy the basis of their traditional foreign policy, questioning both the efficacy and legality of neutrality when squared with the Covenant.[85] Although it might appear that neutrality was incompatible with the obligation of League membership, members, including Norway,[86] *acted as if* neutrality remained an efficacious option, notwithstanding Article XVI and the opinion of many legal analysts.

As has been suggested, then, the post–World War I foreign policy of Norway was largely co-ordinated with the other Scandinavian states, and it was, for the most part,[87] focused on developments in the League of Nations.[88] The policy of Norway (and the Scandinavian states) in the League can be divided roughly into three periods: from 1920 to 1933 and the rise of Hitler and the failure of the disarmament conference; from 1933 to 1936 and the total disillusionment wrought by the Ethiopian crisis and subsequent fiascos; and from 1936 to the outbreak of World War II, during which period Norway attempted to re-establish the prerequisites for a security policy based on strict and traditional neutrality.[89] Though no attempt will be made here to trace to the story of the "Scandinavian bloc" at Geneva, in summary fashion, their individual aims in the League were primarily focused on its legal functions and its jurisdictional base. In this regard, they jointly advocated, supported, and lobbied for (1) universality, (2) a declaration of rights for national minorities, (3) codification of international law, (4) wider competence for the Permanent Court of International Justice, (5) the creation of permanent institutions for inquiry and conciliation, (6) radical reduction of armaments, and (7) increased authority for the League Assembly.

However, the tensions of 1933–36 and the failure of the League to prevent aggression and to provide redress for a wronged small country only confirmed the worst suspicions of the Norwegians about the "politically-inspired" machinations of the great powers and, in their view, the total bankruptcy of collective security. The Italo-Ethiopian War was a turning point, affirming past suspicion and skepticism and "proving" that the League could not provide security to the small states.[90] Earlier Norway had strongly affirmed the "idea" of the League, and had even permitted herself to be drawn into the Ethiopian affair, but by summer of 1936 the leaf was turned: Norway had too much to lose acting as a producer of security and little to gain, in her view of her favorable geographic position, as a consumer of security.[91] In the summer of 1936, Norway declared jointly with six other states [92] that because of the incomplete and inconsistent application of the Covenant and the failure to make progress in disarmament,[93] she no longer felt any obligation to honor the sanctions clauses. This fundamental change of policy was summed up as follows:

> The small powers had entered the League of Nations hoping for general security in a Universal League; but the League was not universal and was not likely to become so, and in a conflict the system might work to the disadvantage of the small states. Thus they wanted recognition of the fact that they no longer considered themselves bound by the obligations of Article 16.[94]

Consequently, Norway, along with the other traditionally neutral states began to discuss new approaches to security. During 1936 many advocated regional pacts for the application of sanctions. Norway, however, opposed regional arrangements. The Norwegian Foreign Minister pointed to the danger of their evolving into military alliances:

> If I said we do not want to see the League of Nations take the shape of a big military alliance, we will still less like to see such alliances arising within the League.[95]

If Norway were not going to be involved in a war under League sponsorship, neither would she be involved through a regional alliance.

In a speech to the Storting in the summer of 1937 the Norwegian Foreign Minister again asserted without equivocation Norwegian freedom of action.

> Norway does not consider herself under any obligation to participate in military sanctions. . . . Article XVI leaves to each state the right decide for itself. . . . Norway is resolved to remain mistress of her own decision in the matter.[96]

In his speech from the Throne in the beginning of 1938 [97] at the opening session of the Storting, the Norwegian King stated that "The task of Norwegian foreign policy must always be to keep the country out of war." [98] That this formulation of policy was supported by the other Scandinavian countries was affirmed in the spring of 1938 when they stated in a joint communiqué [99] that they were unanimous that

Now as before the Northern states ought and desired to remain outside any bloc of powers constituted in Europe, and in case of war between such blocs would do everything in their power not to be drawn into such a war. [100]

Norway, though still in the League, had thus made it absolutely clear by these and subsequent statements [101] that she viewed the sanctions system as both dangerous and meaningless and now looked to neutrality and not collective defense as the basis of her security policy.

The new Norwegian neutrality policy was nonetheless typical: unlike Sweden, Norwegian neutrality manifested itself primarily via verbal declarations. The Norwegian Foreign Minister spoke seldom of military preparations; all that was required was the declaration of one's intention to remain outside of war:

. . . there is one primary condition absolutely indispensable to the possibility of remaining neutral, and that is the *firmly stated will* of the nation, even before the war, to maintain perfect neutrality. [102]

While the Swedes employed military capability and preparedness (what is referred to as "armed neutrality" or "total defense") as a technique to communicate their intentions, the Norwegian Foreign Minister did not attach significance to armaments as a vehicle for communicating political will. Rather, he stated:

the proof of such will is [keeping] clear of all alliances with any bloc of powers forming itself in the world. [103]

Although there is some evidence that the Norwegians probably viewed their geographic position as a depreciating asset, [104] they nevertheless obviously felt sufficiently protected by their physical isolation to decline a proffered non-aggression pact with Berlin in the spring of 1939; [105] the Danes, however, felt unable to refuse and signed.

At the same time, the Norwegian government came under strong domestic criticism, with the opposition parties challenging the wisdom of the unarmed neutrality pursued by the government. In the debate on the Speech from the Throne in February, 1939, the Opposition charged that

the Government has refused to discuss such strengthening of our national defense as is necessitated by considerations for the preservation of neutrality and full independence for the country. [106]

The opposition parties, and especially the Conservatives, fully supported neutrality as a policy, [107] but they did not agree with its implementation: they looked more to the Swedish brand of armed neutrality and rejected the antimilitaristic and pacifistic basis in which the ruling Norwegian Labor party rooted its neutrality. The Conservative Chairman of the Foreign Affairs Committee stated that

Our policy of neutrality cannot be based on the false feeling of security which might result from alliances, but solely on our own willingness and *preparedness* to protect our unconditional neutrality on every side. . . . Our will to neutrality should be mainly *demonstrated by our strengthening the national defense* that we may be *prepared to repel any violation of our territory*. Only thus can we contribute to strengthening the feeling of security in Europe. [108]

This view of neutrality, this concept of communicating political will, and this theory of military capability as stabilizing inputs in international politics were not, however, shared by the Labor party elite and thus were not reflected in Norwegian foreign policy prior to World War II.

Summary.—As the above indicates, Norwegian foreign policy after World War I very actively anticipated transforming the international system, and, when that failed in the late thirties, the Labor government chose non-involvement in the politics among the great powers and a status of non-belligerency—or neutrality, in the event the unwanted war occurred. Their objective corresponding to this latter policy was to persuade the other European powers of their intention not to allow themselves to become involved in the war. The commitments undertaken by the Norwegian leadership to achieve this objective were largely legal and symbolic and took the form of unilateral and multilateral declarations of intentions coupled with protests, once the war began, to the major belligerent powers regarding alleged violations of Norwegian neutral rights. Some commitments of a concrete nature were undertaken. Most dramatic among these was the Norwegian refusal to permit Allied troops to cross Norwegian territory in order to aid the Finns during the winter war [109] and small increments in the defense budgets of 1938–39.[110] In short, the Norwegians were adhering to the admonition of the poet Bjørnson, who had argued that "the best foreign policy is no foreign policy," [111] meaning by this that Norway should avoid political ties to foreign nations as a means of achieving security.[112]

In order to contrast that which follows with this brief overview of Norway's role in world affairs up to the outbreak of World War II, a summary description of the Norwegian strategic image is required.

First, Norway perceived her geographic location as peripheral —in "Europe's quiet corner." Although Norway might become involved in a war for political reasons (e.g., mismanagement of political affairs), Norwegian policy-makers saw no compelling reasons for Norway to become entangled in a "European" war as a consequence of her geographic location.[113] Thus, her geography permitted a policy of non-involvement, for it did not present the problems that had to be faced by countries like Denmark and Belgium.

Second, the important division of the international system was between the small states and the large states. To this image of the international system was attached a valuation dimension: the large states were "politically" oriented and pursued only their own narrow national interests.[114] This evaluation was revealingly expressed by the Norwegian Foreign Minister thusly:

> In Norway the Labor Party had voted against entrance of their country into the League of Nations just because of their distrust of the idealism of the Great Powers. Personally, I had been in favor of trying the experiment of the League, but of course I was aware of the inherent dangers of power policies. . . .[115]

On another occasion, the Foreign Minister wrote, expressing the same idea, that the small neutral bloc at Geneva upheld

> the general principles of international justice as opposed to the considerations of political opportunism urged by most of the Great Powers.[116]

Thus is revealed both the cognitive and affective elements of the image: the international system was composed of the larger, opportunistic states together with the small, justice-seeking states, whose work for peace and the rule of law was often undermined by the power orientation of the large. In short, the small states were, in the Norwegian view, sorts of Latter Day Saints, pleading the cause of rectitude and acting as the collective conscience of the great powers.[117]

This leads to a fourth dimension of the strategic image, the image of process. The Norwegian policy elite perceived a great power "cabal" in which decisions were made by and for the benefit of those nations that possessed large increments of military capability.[118] This process image was not revised during the entire period of Norwegian foreign policy from independence till World War II. However, Norway's attitude toward and response to the process she perceived did undergo fundamental revision. From 1905 until the end of World War I, Norway accepted the "reality" of the great power cabal, best shown by her (unsuccessful) attempts to obtain a great power guarantee and endorsement of her permanent and absolute neutrality. However, Norwegian discussion of, and entry into, the League presaged the change in attitude: Norway now attempted to transform the process she perceived as operational from one governed by considerations of power to one founded on justice, equality, and international law. When this proselytizing attempt to change the rules of international interaction and decision-making failed,[119] Norway announced her withdrawal from the game.

With regard to the events immediately preceding Norwegian involvement in World War II, it should be noted that the Norwegian policy elite perceived the threat to Norway in a generalized manner.[120] In other words, although Norway viewed fascism with unmitigated antipathy, ideological considerations were not highly operational. The Foreign Minister himself noted that moral and material considerations, democratic ideals, and seafaring interests attracted Norway to the side of Great Britain,[121] but these considerations would become controlling *only if* Norway were forced to choose sides, that is, only if Norwegian foreign policy failed. Thus the threat to Norway was war in the system and its concomitant dangers.

Finally, regarding the armaments issue in Norway, the Norwegian Labor party leadership in the government had a negative attitude.[122] The Foreign Minister clearly perceived armaments as a cause of war and felt that Norway had little to gain from increased defense expenditures.[123] It could never be argued that the Labor party leadership viewed armaments as potentially stabilizing as well as destabilizing. Armaments were costly, useless, and dangerous.

Thus, the Norwegians felt relatively safe and were fairly confident of their ability to exercise prudence and properly manage their political relations on a unilateral basis and thereby escape involvement should a war "on the Continent" occur. Norway was a peace-loving, cultured nation with no territorial ambitions nor revanchist motivations.[124] Norway was well-protected by geography and could avoid war by declarations of neutrality and a posture of impartiality. Norway's history had demonstrated this fact: Norway had lived in uninterrupted peace for a century and a quarter, since the seventeen day war with Sweden in 1814. Moreover, Norwegians like Bjørnson and Nansen epitomized the peace movement that had its source in the latter half of the nineteenth century, and, even more recently, the Norwegian government itself had demonstrated its commitment to peaceful relations among nations governed by the rule of law by its acceptance of the PCIJ decision in the Greenland case.[125] In short, the peace traditions of the Norwegian people were extraordinarily deep-rooted and were of such a nature that they would surely be respected by other nations.[126] Indeed, Norway had demonstrated in World War I that even under extreme provocation and the most adverse circumstances she would not permit herself to be drawn into war [127]—just as World War I had demonstrated to Norway that a small nation could maintain peace in the midst of conflict. In short, history and experience had "taught" the Norwegians that peace was divisible, that war was an affair of the great powers into which the small nations need not be drawn if only they exercise prudence, demonstrate will with the proper verbalizations, and intelligently manage their political affairs.

1. The frontier with the U.S.S.R., only 122 miles, is a result of Finnish territorial concessions to the U.S.S.R. in World War II. Norway, thus, is the only original NATO member to share a border with the U.S.S.R. Her boundaries with Sweden and Finland are 1,020 miles and 445 miles respectively. For a good discussion and a detailed map (p. 594) of the Norwegian-Soviet frontier, see Gordon W. East, "The New Soviet Frontier," *Foreign Affairs*, XXIX (July, 1951), 595–96.

2. Often referred to in English as Spitzbergen, it is important primarily because of its strategic location in the Arctic Ocean on the northern route from the Soviet Union to the North Atlantic and as a consequence of its coal deposits, the only major deposits to which Norway has access. See John J. Teal, "Europe's Northernmost Frontier," *Foreign Affairs*, XXIX (January, 1951), 263–75; and Trygve Mathisen, *Svalbard in the Changing Arctic* (Oslo: Gyldendal, 1954), chaps. vi, vii.

3. Norway proper has a total area of 125,064 square miles; her two Arctic possessions, Svalbard and Jan Mayen added to her two Antarctic possessions, Peter I Island and Bouvet Island, total more than 24,000 square miles. On these points see Axel Sømme, *A Geography of Norden* (Oslo: J. W. Cappelens Forlag, 1961), pp. 288–91; and Elisabeth Lundevall and Per Hagen, *Facts about Norway* (Oslo: Chr. Schibsteds Forlag, 1964), p. 3.

4. Sømme, *op. cit.*, p. 236.

5. There is one minority group, the Lapps, with an estimated population of 20,000–25,000. This group, however, is isolated in the northern part of the

country and has its own language and cultural traditions. It is a minority group which is receiving more attention in Norway as a result of humanitarian and domestic political considerations as well as in consideration of their position in strategic northern Norway.

6. Norway is divided into five distinct geographical regions: Østlandet, Sørlandet, Vestlandet, Trøndelag, and Nord Norge. East Norway is an agricultural and industrial area, largely urban in composition. The capital, Oslo, is located in this region. South Norway is largely agricultural and rural. West Norway is dominated by Norway's second largest city, Bergen, and is a fishing and fish processing center, although it is rapidly becoming a manufacturing center. Trøndelag, lying in the north-central region of the country, and north Norway are the most sparsely populated regions and are dominated by fishing and agricultural enterprises. There are great variations among all of these regions, especially in language and in cultural and political values. See James A. Storing, *Norwegian Democracy* (Oslo: Universitetsforlaget, 1963), pp. 4–11; Harry Ekstein, *Division and Cohesion in Democracy: A Study of Norway* (Princeton: Princeton University Press, 1966), esp. chaps. iii, iv; and Sømme, *op. cit.*, pp. 238–44, 283–86.

7. Efforts are continually being made to provide incentives to people to settle in the regions other than the Oslofjord area. For example, subsidies are provided to fishermen, in part, to help keep the coastal areas inhabited; industrial enterprises are constructed inland with government subsidies to encourage a more stable population distribution (even though they may operate at less than maximum efficiency); and internal communications systems are under improvement, ranging from a more extensive and efficient railway system to expansion of the state-owned and operated television in the remote regions—even traveling theaters and ministerial-level politicians are venturing into the isolated areas.

8. A terminological issue should be settled here. The term *Scandinavia* is often employed loosely, referring to various groupings of the countries of Northern Europe. The term *Scandinavia* shall be employed herein to denote only Norway, Denmark, and Sweden, while the term *Fenno-Scandinavia* will be used in reference to Norway, Denmark, Sweden, and Finland. The term *Nordic* should be used only in reference to the peoples and socio-cultural aspects of the five Nordic countries, i.e., Fenno-Scandinavia plus Iceland, and the term *Norden* is normally used by political geographers to refer to the region of the Nordic countries. The term *Scandinavian peninsula* is employed only to denote the area occupied by Sweden and Norway. On these points see Sømme, *op. cit.*, pp. 11–17.

9. Walter Fitzgerald, *The New Europe: An Introduction to Its Political Geography* (New York: Harper, 1946), pp. 39–44.

10. See, for example, Karen Larsen, *A History of Norway* (Princeton: Princeton University Press, 1948), pp. 208–40, 343–95, 484–95; John Midgaard, *A Brief History of Norway* (Oslo: Johan Grundt Forlag, 1963), pp. 46–104; and Franz Wendt, *The Nordic Council and Cooperation in Scandinavia* (Copenhagen: Munksgaard, 1959), chap. i.

11. Elias Wessen, "The Scandinavian Community of Language," *Le Nord*, IV (1941), 221–36. Gunnar Leistikow, "Cooperation between the Scandinavian Countries," in Henning Friis (ed.), *Scandinavia between East and West* (Ithaca: Cornell University Press, 1950), pp. 308–10, suggests that while the kinship among the Scandinavian countries is less intense than

nationalism and allegiance to the individual countries, it is nevertheless stronger than the feeling which persists among Anglo-Saxons. Leistikow further hypothesizes that the "community of speech seems to be the root idea of kinship and solidarity, [and] one of the basic elements of Scandinavianism."

12. Norwegian agriculture is very inefficient, and there are no great tracts of fertile farmland; only 43 farms have more than 250 acres. Norway is self-sufficient in livestock products (although feed-stuffs must be imported) and in eggs, butter, cheese, and milk.

13. The primary imports are bread grain, textiles, fuels, metals, machinery, and ships. The shipyards of Sweden, West Germany, Great Britain, and Japan provide the bulk of the Norwegian fleet.

14. The Norwegian shipping fleet totals over fifteen million gross tons, or 10 per cent of the world's tonnage of 140 million gross tons. Thus, Norway ranks fourth after Britain, the U.S., and Liberia. On a per capita basis, Norway has the world's largest shipping fleet. More than 90 per cent of the fleet is engaged in international trade and nearly one-half the tonnage is in tankers, the strategic value of which was evident (especially for Great Britain) in World War II.

15. Norway is especially sensitive to the disadvantages created by flag discrimination, a practice which gives a nation's own ships certain preferences over ships of other nations, apart from considerations of cost or efficiency. Norway will always be found protesting such departures from the principles of free competition in international shipping, as in the case of the U.S. and Soviet agreement regarding wheat shipments in U.S. bottoms. Norwegian shipping requires access to international markets, which flag discrimination limits.

16. For a good yet brief discussion of the structure of the Norwegian economy see Ole Knudsen, *Norway* (Oslo: Ministry of Foreign Affairs, 1964), *passim*, which deals entirely with the major sectors of the Norwegian economy.

17. An English text of the Constitution can be found, along with other documents related to the Constitution in Tønnes Andenaes (ed.), *The Constitution of Norway* (Oslo: Norwegian Universities Press, 1962).

18. See Raymond E. Lindgren, *Norway-Sweden: Union, Disunion, and Scandinavian Integration* (Princeton: Princeton University Press, 1959), pp. 8–131, for perhaps the best treatment in English of the political aspects of the Union period.

19. The supremacy of the Storting was achieved in 1884 with the acceptance by Swedish King Oscar II of the principle that the Norwegian Cabinet should enjoy the continuing confidence of the legislative organ. See, for example, T. K. Derry, *A Short History of Norway* (London: George Allen and Unwin, 1960), pp. 173–80; and Kristian Bloch, *Kongens Råd* (Oslo: Universitetsforlaget, 1963), pp. 15–21.

20. The Storting is elected as a single group, afterward dividing itself for legislative purposes into the Lagting and the Odelsting, with one-fourth serving in the former and the remaining three-fourths serving in the latter "chamber." See Storing, *op. cit.*, chap. v.

21. One of the unique features of the Norwegian parliamentary system is the absence of a royal dissolution authority. That the term of parliament is

fixed is a potentially destabilizing feature of the Norwegian system of government, especially when, as was the case after the 1961 elections, the government's parliamentary support is tenuous.

22. See Appendix A.

23. For a good discussion of the ideological and policy commitments of the various Norwegian political parties see Storing, *op. cit.*, pp. 135–43. For a discussion dealing only with the bourgeois parties see Sven Groennings, "Cooperation among Norway's Non-Socialist Political Parties" (unpublished Ph.D. dissertation, Stanford University, 1962). See Henry Valen and Daniel Katz, *Political Parties in Norway*, (Oslo: Universitetsforlaget, 1964), pp. 22–41 for the development of the Norwegian party system.

24. For a discussion of the Norwegian Communist party, see Jahn Otto Johansen's chapter on Norway in William E. Griffith (ed.), *Communism In Europe*, Vol. II, (Cambridge: M. I. T. Press, 1966), pp. 321–69. On the Socialist People's party see Finn Gustavsen, "Utenrikspolitikken i Foregrunnen" in Per Øyvind Heradstveit's *Partiene og utenrikspolitikken* (Oslo: Aschehoug, 1965), pp. 65–78.

25. The most heated discussion of foreign policy since Norway joined the Atlantic alliance came in 1961–62 on the question of Norway's application to the Common Market. The Storting finally approved the application, but there were thirty-seven dissenting votes, primarily from the Socialist People's party and the Center party with a few dissident votes from Labor, Liberals, and the Christian People's party.

26. Storing, *op. cit.*, p. 221; Valen and Katz, *op. cit.*, pp. 31–32. The Communist party is not mentioned here since it has no parliamentary representation.

27. Halvdan Koht (1935–41), Trygve Lie (1941–46), and Halvard Lange (1946–65). Exception is made to the short interregnum in the fall of 1963 when the Conservatives led a coalition government for less than a month. National elections were held in the fall of 1965, however, and ended thirty years of Labor rule in Norway. The new government was formed in October, 1965, headed by the Center party with Conservative John Lyng serving as Foreign Minister.

28. General (administrative), Political (subdivided into five functional offices), Trade, Protocol, Law, Press, and Cultural Relations.

29. See Storing, *op. cit.*, pp. 109–12 for a brief discussion of recruitment, appointment, and training practices in the Norwegian Foreign Service. For a discussion of the history of the Norwegian Foreign Service see Reidar Omang, *Utenrikstjenesten*, (Oslo: Utenriksdepartementet, 1954).

30. Erik Colban, *Stortinget og Utenrikspolitikken* (Oslo: Universitetsforlaget, 1961), pp. 18–48; normally the Storting committees reflect the political balance of the Storting itself; however, in the critical 1948–49 period Communists were excluded from the Foreign Affairs Committee even though they had eleven members in the parliament. For a discussion in English of parliamentary participation and control in the area of foreign policy see Einar Løchen, *Norway in European and Atlantic Cooperation* (Oslo: Universitetsforlaget, 1964), pp. 67–83. For an explication of the constitutional competence of the Storting in foreign policy see Einar Løchen and Rolf N. Torgersen, *Norway's Views on Sovereignty* (Bergen: Chr. Michelsens' Institutt, 1955), pp. 13–20.

31. "The fact that there is an enlarged Foreign Relations Committee strengthens the possibility of parliamentary control over the government's foreign policy. It is also of importance for the government to have such a committee, where it is able to talk more freely on confidential or secret matters than is the case in open sessions of the Storting. The Committee may be used by the government as a sounding-board for new ideas on foreign policy. No votes or decisions are taken by the committee, and the constitutional responsibility of the government for conducting foreign policy is not affected."—Løchen, op. cit., p. 69.

32. The power of the governing party in foreign affairs is substantial. In the postwar era there have been wide divergencies between the Labor party leadership and its rank-and-file on foreign policy questions. According to Valen and Katz, op. cit., pp. 87–88, "It is highly probable that if the stand of the national leadership on membership in NATO or on the rearmament of Germany had been put to the test of a referendum of all Labor party members, substantial majorities would have been registered against the position of the national leaders." However, the government party's near-monopoly of information and its concomitant ability to "pose the problem and define the issue [make] it difficult for the membership organization to assert its own wishes."

33. Larsen, op. cit., pp. 243–369; and Derry, op. cit., pp. 68–108. Between 1319 and 1360 a personal union existed between Norway and Sweden. Norway and Denmark were united in 1380 in a union which lasted until 1814. During this period the two were joined by Sweden from 1397 until 1521 in the so-called Kalmar Union.

34. The impact of the Napoleonic Wars on Northern Europe was clearly expressed by Franz Wendt, op. cit., pp. 17–19, where he states, "The cataclysm caused by the Napoleonic wars was one of the most important and revolutionary events in the history of the Nordic peoples. It severed ancient ties and became the starting point of entirely new developments."

35. Reference here is to Marshall Jean Baptiste Bernadotte, elected Crown Prince Karl Johan on November 10, 1810, and who, in 1818, became King Karl XIV Johan of Sweden.

36. Rowland Kenney, The Northern Tangle (London: J. M. Dent, 1946), pp. 31–32, 37–39.

37. See Lindgren, op. cit., pp. 8–28, for a good discussion of the formation of the Union; see also Magnus Jensen, Norges Historie: Unionstiden 1814–1905 (Oslo: Universitetsforlaget, 1963), III, 11–32.

38. The Norwegian position was stated as follows by Kenney, op. cit., p. 42: ". . . the Treaty of Kiel, with its demand for the transference of their national allegiance from one power to another, infuriated the Norwegians. King Frederik VI of Denmark might absolve them of their oath of allegiance to him; but they refused to acknowledge his right to call upon them to be loyal to a king of another country. If the Danish king renounced his sovereignty, it reverted to the Norwegian people, and it was for them to decide upon whom it should be bestowed. The Treaty of Kiel, they said, was invalid so far as they were concerned."

39. For the best short discussion in English of the intellectual and historical roots as well as the development of the Norwegian Constitution see Frede Castberg, Norway and the Western Powers (London: George Allen and Unwin, 1957), pp. 5–24; see also Frede Castberg, Norges Statsforfatning

(Oslo: Arbeidernes Aktietrykkeri, 1947) for the most authoritative book on constitutional law in Norway; Larsen, *op. cit.*, chap. xv; Storing, *op. cit.*, pp. 20–26.

40. Reference here is to the Moss Convention of August 14, 1814.

41. October 7, 1814.

42. November 4, 1814.

43. Kenney, *op. cit.*, p. 43.

44. For perhaps the best discussion in English of this period see Lindgren, *op. cit.*, pp. 29–111; see also Kenney, *op. cit.*, pp. 44–49; and Jensen, *op. cit.*, Vol. III.

45. Kenney, *op. cit.*, p. 44.

46. After more than a decade of fruitless negotiations, Norwegian independence from the Union with Sweden was effected on June 7, 1905. The separation was given legal status through the Treaty of Karlstad. The issue of a separate and independent consular service was raised as early as 1830 by the Norwegians. On this see Lindgren, *op. cit.*, pp. 47–48. For the most concise statement of the Norwegian position during the dissolution crisis see the letter by Dr. Fridtjof Nansen to the *Times* (London), March 25, 1905.

47. Derry, *op. cit.*, p. 161 states, "The cardinal event in the entire history of the Norwegian mercantile marine is undoubtedly the repeal of the British Navigation Acts. This threw open the trade of the whole British Empire to free competition for freights; and inaugurated a long period in which flag discrimination was out of fashion."

48. For an excellent and scholarly treatment of the pan-Scandinavian movement and Norway's role in it see Theodore Jorgenson, *Norway's Relation to Scandinavian Unionism, 1815–1871* (Northfield, Minnesota: St. Olaf College Press, 1935), *passim*.

49. Lindgren, *op. cit.*, p. 49, states, "The failure of Norway-Sweden to aid the Danish cause in the war with Prussia in 1863–1864 killed political Scandinavianism." For a good yet brief discussion of the complex Schleswig-Holstein problem and its effect both in Denmark and on the Scandinavian movement see Kenney, *op. cit.*, pp. 58–63.

50. For a good discussion of joint actions undertaken by organizations established by the Scandinavians, on both public and private bases, see Eric Bellquist, "Inter-Scandinavian Cooperation," *The Annals*, CLXVIII (July, 1933), 183–96; and Wendt, *op. cit.*, pp. 22–27.

51. John H. Wuorinen, "Problems of a Scandinavian Bloc," *Current History*, XVI (January, 1949), 12.

52. It was during a highpoint in the Scandinavian movement that King Oscar I, in June of 1856, made the now famous statement that (with the exception of the last sentence) remains a truism in Scandinavian relations: "Henceforth a war between Scandinavian brothers is an impossibility. This irrevocable decision is imprinted with indelible letters in the hearts of the two Northern kings and in the bosoms of the three Northern peoples . . . Our swords stand ready for mutual defense."—Bellquist, *op. cit.*, p. 183.

53. On this point, and for a provocative general discussion of Norwegian nationalism, see Andreas Elviken, "The Genesis of Norwegian Nationalism," *Journal of Modern History*, III (September, 1931), 391.

54. Reference here is to Bjørnstjerne Bjørnson.

55. Later, in 1897, prior to the meeting of the first Hague Conference, the Storting passed a similar resolution, this time without dissent. See Midgaard, *op. cit.,* pp. 98–99.

56. The increasingly active role played by Norway in the interest of international law and adjudication was given recognition by the Swedish industrialist Alfred Nobel, who, in his will, designated the Norwegian Storting to award an annual prize to that individual who had made a contribution to the work toward peace. (The Storting, which appoints a committee to award the Nobel Peace Prize, made its first award in 1901.)

57. Nils Ørvik, *The Decline of Neutrality* (Oslo: Johan Grundt Tanum Forlag, 1953), p. 29. Norway was aiming toward general international recognition of its permanent neutrality, a goal achieved by only three countries in the nineteenth century: Switzerland in 1815, Belgium in 1839, and Luxembourg in 1867.

58. See Kenney, *op. cit.,* pp. 50–51. The Treaty Guaranteeing the Territorial Integrity of Norway (November 2, 1907) infuriated the Swedes, who charged that, under the circumstances, the Treaty could only be directed at them. Although the Norwegian government repudiated these charges, the Swedes' deep resentment was evidenced in December of the same year when they denied permission to a special Norwegian delegation to attend the funeral of King Oscar II. (Norway repudiated the Treaty in 1924.)

59. Franklin Scott, *The United States and Scandinavia* (Cambridge: Harvard University Press, 1950), pp. 211–12.

60. *Ibid.,* p. 211.

61. Reidar Omang, "Fifty years of Norwegian Foreign Policy," *Norseman,* (May-June, 1955), p. 154.

62. Nils Ørvik, *Trends in Norwegian Foreign Policy* (Oslo: Norwegian Institute of International Affairs, 1962), pp. 4–5.

63. See Kenney, *op. cit.,* pp. 51–52, for a discussion of the German interest in the Norwegian coastal areas and of the writings of German military leaders (especially the writings of General Bernhardi) expressing the need for German control of southern coastal areas of Norway in the event of a war with England.

64. See on these points, Wilhelm Keilhau, "Britain and Norway: A Survey of Mutual Relations," *Norseman,* XI (January-February, 1953), 1–9; and Maurice Michael, *Haakon, King of Norway* (New York: Macmillan, 1958), chap. i.

65. In 1911 the Inter-Parliamentary Union expanded its functions to the preparation of joint legislation in the areas of social and economic policies.

66. Bellquist, *op. cit.,* p. 185 states, "The suspicions which prevailed in Scandinavia, particularly between Sweden and Norway, prior to the outbreak of the World War were, of course, primarily due to the Union conflicts and dissolution of 1905. They were also founded on Sweden's fear that Norway might be forced to join the Entente because of her great dependence upon England. Thus the Swedes envisaged their country surrounded by two enemies, Russia and Norway, supported by England."

67. On the subject of Scandinavian co-operation in the political field just prior to the war see Bellquist, *op. cit.,* pp. 185–86.

68. Scott, *op. cit.*, p. 216; Kenney, *op. cit.*, p. 66.

69. December 18, 1914.

70. In these actions the Scandinavian countries were the only group attempting concentrated measures in support of a common policy. After the outbreak of war, the positions taken by the governments in their respective statements of policy were affirmed by the Northern Inter-Parliamentary Union, in November of 1914. See Bellquist, *op. cit.*, p. 185.

71. Generally, the joint statements issued by the Scandinavians were composed in the Swedish chancery under the skilled guidance of Swedish Prime Minister Hjalmar Hammarskjöld, who was, unlike his Norwegian counterpart, trained and experienced in international law. See Scott, *op. cit.*, p. 216.

72. Finn Moe, *Norge i den nye Verden* (Oslo: Tiden Norsk Forlag, 1946), p. 17.

73. Julius Moritzen, "The Perils of Scandinavia," *North American Review*, CCV (February, 1917), 229.

74. Rolf Thommessen, *Norges Utenrikspolitikk under Verdenskrigen* (Kristiana: Tiden, 1917), p. 4.

75. Arne Ording, "Norsk Utenrikspolitikk," in Sverre Steen (ed.), *Norges Krig*, I (Oslo: Glydendal, 1947), pp. 51–52.

76. Paul G. Vigness, *The Neutrality of Norway in the World War* (Stanford: Stanford University Press, 1932), p. 172.

77. Ørvik, *The Decline of Neutrality*, p. 50.

78. *Ibid.*, p. 50.

79. *Ibid.*, pp. 59–61; see also Olav Riste, *The Neutral Ally* (Oslo: Universitetsforlaget, 1965), *passim*.

80. Løchen and Torgersen, *op. cit.*, pp. 24–31; also Bellquist, *op. cit.*, p. 187. A private Norwegian Association for the League of Nations, under the leadership of Fridtjof Nansen, came forth with similar views in 1919, although Nansen later supported the League even though it was founded on principles which differed fundamentally from those he earlier advocated.

81. For the most authoritative examination of the Scandinavian states in the League, see S. Shepard Jones, *The Scandinavian States in the League of Nations* (Princeton: Princeton University Press, 1939). On this point see Thomas Hovet, Jr., *Bloc Politics in the U.N.* (Cambridge: Harvard University Press, 1960), p. 73, who also cites the concerted efforts of the "Scandinavian bloc" at Geneva.

82. Denmark was most enthusiastic about the League, affirming unanimously in the Rigsdag the decision to join. The vote in the Norwegian Storting was 100–20, while the least enthusiasm was evidenced in Sweden, where the Riksdag voted affirmatively 86–47 and 152–67 respectively in its upper and lower houses. Finland (which had just gained its independence from Russia in 1917) and Iceland became members in 1920 and 1925.

83. Scott, *op. cit.*, p. 225. The Norwegian Labor party had, in 1919, joined the Third International. The majority then voted to withdraw in 1923, and those who remained formed the core of the Norwegian Communist party. On this see Johansen, *op. cit.*, Kenney, *op. cit.*, p. 90; and Arvo Tuominen,

"The Northern Countries and Communism," *Norseman,* XII (July-August, 1954), 217–29.

84. Brita Skottsberg Åhman, "Scandinavian Foreign Policy, Past and Present," in Henning Friis, *op. cit.,* p. 266. Copyright 1950 by Cornell University. Used by permission of Cornell University Press.

85. See Ørvik, *The Decline of Neutrality,* Part III, for a thorough discussion of the various views regarding the doctrine of neutrality and the obligations of members of the League of Nations. Ørvik argues, after analyzing various points of view, that traditionally defined neutrality was incompatible with the League. However, in view of the assumptions made herein regarding foreign policy, what is important is what the Norwegians *thought to be true,* and in this instance they did not agree with the opinions of many legal analysts.

86. Norway, from the beginning, refused to recognize Article XVI as obligatory. On this see Løchen and Torgersen, *op. cit.,* pp. 27–32.

87. One event of some significance did occur outside the confines of the League. Although Norway was not a participant in the war, she did profit territorially when in 1919 the Peace Conference conferred on Norway sovereignty over the Svalbard archipelago, political control over which had been disputed for decades by Norway, Sweden, and Russia. Svalbard was incorporated "As part of the Kingdom of Norway" on August 14, 1925, when the Soviet Union finally ratified the Treaty of 1920. Norway's sovereignty over the area is limited, for the terms of the Treaty guarantee the subjects of the signatory powers equal access to the territory's resources, and the territory must remain demilitarized. See Mathisen, *op. cit.,* pp. 11–16.

88. The Scandinavian states, however, did not act as a formal bloc, nor should the co-operation which existed be over-emphasized. The Scandinavian ministers discovered early (at a Ministerial meeting in Copenhagen in August of 1920) that general agreement existed on the basic issues in their foreign policies. Although during this period the issue of a Scandinavian alliance was raised often in the press and elsewhere, it was never seriously considered by the governments. In fact, in 1923 the Swedish Foreign Minister, apparently on his own initiative, proposed a defense union with Finland and was quickly forced to resign. In July, 1921, *Göteborgs handels och sjöfartstidning,* one of Scandinavia's most influential newspapers, wrote that there should be "no illusions concerning Scandinavian co-operation, which may prove as brittle as glass on being subjected to the slightest strain. Scandinavian cooperation in foreign politics is problematic, even within the most restricted limits." To support the assertion that too much can be made of intra-Scandinavian co-operation at the government level, it can be pointed out that the annual ministerial meetings, which had been so important in Scandinavian political life for almost a decade, were allowed to lapse with the August, 1920, meeting cited above, not to be resumed until January, 1932. On these points see Herbert Tingsten, *Debate on the Foreign Policy of Sweden, 1918–1939* (New York: Oxford University Press), pp. 137–48; Kenney, *op. cit.,* p. 101.

89. See Jones, *op. cit., passim.*

90. Halvdan Koht, *Norway Neutral and Invaded* (London: Hutchinson, 1941), pp. 14–15. Koht states that when the League met in September of 1936, the delegates of the small states frankly and unambiguously expressed to

the other delegates their new attitude toward the League. "Such was the influence of events in international politics upon the attitude of all the small nations of Europe, and thus they were preparing the Great Powers for the policy of neutrality."

91. Jones, *op. cit.*, p. 217.

92. The declaration was made by the Foreign Ministers of Finland, Denmark, Norway, Sweden, Switzerland, The Netherlands, and Republican Spain meeting at Geneva on July 1, 1936.

93. Koht, "Problems of Neutrality," *Le Nord*, II (1939), 132, states that in his view the only basis for a favorable development of the League would have been progress in disarmament. See also Jones, *op. cit.*, pp. 217–51.

94. Ørvik, *The Decline of Neutrality*, p. 177.

95. Koht, "Problems of Neutrality," p. 135.

96. *Ibid.*, p. 133. The date was June 24, 1937. The Swedish Foreign Minister Sandler made essentially the same declaration in the Riksdag on January 17, 1938.

97. January 13, 1938.

98. Quoted by Koht, "Problems of Neutrality," p. 134.

99. The communiqué was issued following a ministerial meeting in Oslo on April 5–6, 1938 attended by Finland, Norway, Sweden, and Denmark.

100. Koht, "Problems of Neutrality," p. 134.

101. With reference to the King's statement (cited above) the Storting unanimously declared on May 31, 1938, that "it maintained the right of the country to observe complete and absolute neutrality in any war that it would not itself recognize as constituting an action of the League of Nations." It should be noted that this formulation of the resolution did not foreclose for Norway the option of joining in a League sanctioned action if it so chose; nevertheless the thrust of the resolution was the assertion of freedom to choose. The following day the Swedish Riksdag made a similar declaration, and in July the Oslo Powers (Finland, the Scandinavian states, and the Low countries) meeting in Copenhagen issued a similar communiqué. See Koht, "Problems of Neutrality," p. 134; Koht, *Norway Neutral and Invaded*, p. 14; and Ørvik, *The Decline of Neutrality, op. cit.*, pp. 185–87.

102. Koht, "Problems of Neutrality," p. 136. (Italics added.)

103. *Ibid.*

104. Halvdan Koht, "Neutrality and Peace: The View of a Small Power," *Foreign Affairs*, XV (January, 1937), 281.

105. The pact was offered on April 28, 1939, and rejected on Norway's Independence Day (May 17) because, in the Foreign Minister's words, "non-aggression treaties with distant countries would seem to obtain a political character that might come in conflict with strict neutrality." Sweden also declined. See Koht, "Problems of Neutrality," p. 137. (Italics added.)

106. "Chronique Trimestrille," *Le Nord*, II (1939), 118–19. The Labor government, headed by Prime Minister Nygaardsvold, defeated this motion designed to force the government to meet with other parliamentary leaders for the purpose of discussing an increase in the defense effort.

107. The leader of the Conservative party, C. J. Hambro, was also President of the Storting and Chairman of the Foreign Affairs and Constitution Committee. His support of neutrality is beyond question. Referring to the concern expressed in the British Parliament for the security of the Northern countries and the possibility of British protection, Hambro stated on March 19, 1939, that "we appreciate highly the sympathy for the Northern countries which underlie such declarations, but we have not asked for any such guarantee from any power or group of powers, nor do we want it. . . . Today our faith in promises of help from great powers is more limited than it ever has been . . . a neutrality quaranteed from one quarter, ceases to be neutrality if the case should arise." See *Ibid.*, pp. 250–51.

108. *Ibid.* (Italics added.)

109. For the Norwegian view see Koht, *Norway Neutral and Invaded*, pp. 34–42; for a discussion from the point of view of the Allies and their desire to secure Scandinavia for both economic and strategic reasons, their fear of provoking the U.S.S.R., and their problems with the Scandinavians see William L. Langer and S. Everett Gleason, *The Challenge to Isolation: 1937–1940* (New York: Harper, 1952), pp. 376–85; and J. R. H. Butler, *Grand Strategy*, I (London: Butler & Tanner, 1957), 91–150.

110. Norwegian defense expenditures were cut radically in 1922, and this low level of appropriation (at times about one-half of the pre-1914 expenditure) continued until the mid-1930's. From 1936 to 1938 there was a gradual increase, and in 1939 extraordinary funds were requested and granted by the Storting, although even in these instances the Conservatives introduced substitute motions which called for much greater sacrifices for defense. See Nils Ørvik, *Sikkerhetspolitikken 1920–1939*, II (Oslo: Johan Grundt Tanum, 1961), 456–57; "Chronique Trimestrille," *Le Nord*, II (1939), 537–39, 541; and Koht, *Norway Neutral and Invaded*, pp. 17–19.

111. Reidar Omang, *op. cit.*, p. 154.

112. Koht, "Neutrality and Peace," p. 280.

113. Koht, *Norway Neutral and Invaded*, pp. 26–27, argues that the danger to Norwegian neutrality (i.e., non-involvement) had diminished from the point of view of strategy. "During the past twenty years the technique of war had developed to such a perfection that none of the belligerents nearest to Norway, neither Germany nor Great Britain, would feel such a pressing need of occupying certain places in Norway as bases of attack against the enemy either by sea or air. Each of them would be able to grapple with the other from their own country."

114. Koht, "Problems of Neutrality," p. 129 wrote: "Justice seems to have become an obsolete word in international affairs, collective organization of the nations is an antiquated ideal. National strength is frankly proclaimed as the true basis for the rights of each nation (and) the desires of the great powers come anew to the front, or, to put it more accurately, that the Great Powers primarily consider their national interests."

115. *Ibid.*, p. 131.

116. Koht, "Neutrality and Peace," pp. 287–88.

117. Ahman, *op. cit.* Norway expressed this attitude in recommendations for amending the roles of the League Council and Assembly, and the attempts made to exploit fully the provisions of Article XIX of the Covenant. See Jones,

op. cit., 95–105. Also revealing is a statement by Koht in 1937: "If the small states declared themselves unwilling or unable to accept the military obligations for purposes of international justice or peace, the question arises whether it is safe to leave the military defense of the principles of the League of Nations to the great powers alone. That seems to be the only alternative. But I think it fair to say that such a *delegation* of power to a limited group of strongly armed states will awake much mistrust all around the world. In the various conflicts which have occurred inside the League of Nations we have seen the great powers acting in furtherance of their own interests (and) it has been disillusioning to the small states to see how often the question of the balance of power has influenced the great nations when they must make decisions regarding the maintenance of international relations."—Koht, "Neutrality and Peace," p. 288.

118. It is interesting to note here a historical event which has been so important to contemporary international politics, Munich, and Norway's evaluation. Munich probably symbolizes to most Americans the futility of "appeasement" or compromise with one's adversary. Likewise Munich was more than an isolated historical event to the Norwegian Foreign Minister, but to him it symbolized the "fact" that the great powers will sacrifice the small where the vital interests of the great are involved. See Koht, *Norway Neutral and Invaded*, pp. 13–14. The Conservative Foreign Affairs Committee Chairman stated, expressing the same evaluation, "Then after Munich I took a very strong stand against the policy it sanctifies . . . and publicly uttered the opinion that after the Munich Agreement no small nation could be sure of continued independent national life." See C. J. Hambro, *I Saw It Happen in Norway* (New York: Appleton-Century, 1940), p. 73.

119. Reference here is to the many efforts made by Norway in the League on behalf of compulsory arbitration, adjudication, and disarmament. See Jones, *op. cit.*, *passim*.

120. Ørvik, *Sikkerhetspolitikken: 1920–1939*, pp. 455, 460.

121. Koht, *Norway Neutral and Invaded*, p. 41.

122. *Ibid.*, pp. 17–19.

123. *Ibid.*, pp. 16–19; and Koht "Neutrality and Peace," p. 289. Koht maintained that rearmament was a "hateful thing" and the Norwegian leaders "had been well aware how the rivalry of rearmament had always been leading nations into war." See also Jones, *op. cit.*, pp. 217–51.

124. Koht, "Neutrality and Peace," p. 281.

125. For the background to the Danish Norwegian dispute see L. Preuss, "The Dispute between Denmark and Norway over the Sovereignty of East Greenland," *American Journal of International Law*, XXVI (July, 1932), 469–87. The PCIJ determined in April, 1933, that Denmark retained valid title to all of Greenland. The Aaland Islands controversy between Sweden and Finland was settled in June of 1921 by the League Council with the award of sovereignty to Finland. For a general discussion of the political dimensions of both controversies see Åhman, *op. cit.*, pp. 263–64, 270–71; Kenney, *op. cit.*, pp. 86, 93–94.

126. Koht, *Norway Neutral and Invaded*, pp. 15–17.

127. Vigness, *op. cit.*, p. 172.

CHAPTER II

The Emergence of New Axioms in Norwegian Foreign Policy

World War II and the London government.—Following the German invasion [1] in the morning of April 9, 1940,[2] the government and the Storting fled the capital after having rejected a German ultimatum [3] demanding Norwegian co-operation in the German occupation of the country.[4] The King and the government carried on the struggle in Norway against the Germans until June,[5] when they were finally forced to flee the country and establish a government-in-exile in London. Although this two-month period is very interesting in itself, two developments relevant to subsequent outcomes of Norwegian foreign policy are important.

The first involved the establishment of the legal base for the government in London. Before the government left Norway, the Storting granted the Council of State, i.e., the King and his ministers, full powers to govern the country for the duration of the war. This was achieved through the instrument of the so-called Elverum Authorization of Full Powers [6] and was further necessitated by a provision of the Norwegian Constitution which prohibits the King, without parliamentary consent, from residing outside the kingdom for more than six months.[7] Thus, some weeks later, when the government established itself in London, in possession of the total gold reserves of the Bank of Norway and in control of the fourth largest merchant fleet in the world, its legal basis was solid; and its international status was enhanced when it was accorded full diplomatic status by the British.[8]

The second development involves the impact made on government leaders by the absence of military preparations and of prior provision for external aid in case of international conflict. Although the British immediately pledged aid to Norway, it was not until mid-April that Allied troops were on Norwegian soil.[9] Had external military assistance been more readily available or had the government more adequately provided for its domestic military capability, there is a possibility that a neutral zone could have been established in north Norway, thereby permitting the government to remain on Norwegian soil. As it was, the negotiations on this matter with the Germans dissolved as the Norwegian military position deteriorated rapidly. This first-hand experience of the utility of military power gained by the political leaders during the early months of the German-Norwegian war left impressions and attitudes to which reference would be made often in the years to come.

The government had established itself in London by the mid-summer of 1940, succeeded in gaining recognition from other states, and proved to be financially stable and independent.[10] Although it is often asserted that Norwegian foreign policy had changed fundamentally with the German invasion, this view is somewhat superficial and misleading. Once Norway's neutrality had been irrevocably compromised, Norway's prewar foreign policy had, of course, been willy-nilly altered. And once the government decided to resist the German invasion and, later, to carry on the war from London, Norwegian foreign policy became functionally related to the requirements of liberation. However these changes, as far as foreign policy is concerned, reflect more decisions made by others (i.e., the Germans) than decisions made by Norwegians. In fact, Foreign Minister Koht retained his position in the Foreign Office in London,[11] and there is nothing to indicate that his views of Norway's role in world affairs had been altered in any way beyond the tactical requirements imposed by the determination of the government to cooperate with others in the liberation of Norway from the Germans.

The Foreign Minister was soon to encounter resistance, however, as foreign ministers whose policies have failed so often do. Most important was the continued disagreement, soon to become disenchantment, with Koht among a hard-core element [12] of the Norwegian government and politically relevant elite in exile. Several prominent members of the Norwegian community in London were advocating a more active foreign policy, and in July of 1940 they petitioned the government to promulgate and pursue a more vigorous and well-defined policy. In a later petition they requested the government to sign an alliance with the United Kingdom, to clarify Norwegian aims in the war, and to take measures to build up the morale of the home front.[13]

These petitions represented frontal assaults on Koht's foreign policy, but he stood his ground and in September of 1940 strongly defended his policy and denied the efficacy of closer ties with the Allies in the form of an alliance with Great Britain. Koht's basic position was the same as prior to the war: the great powers would determine the peace, and in this determination there was no room for the small powers. Regarding the liberation, his view was that the British had great incentives to expel Germany from Norway; thus a treaty with the U.K. was at best redundant. In addition, Koht was fearful that a close alignment between Norway and Great Britain could be injurious to Norwegian relations with the U.S.S.R., a country, in his view, also having an interest in preventing another great power's influence in the North.[14]

The Foreign Minister's position was substantially undermined in November of 1940 when the Norwegian Cabinet decided unanimously that an agreement should be made with the U.K. to insure Norwegian independence and freedom after the war,[15] and for all practical purposes this vote marked the end of Koht's leadership and influence in Norwegian foreign policy. He continued to adhere to the old doctrines of neutrality and the dogmas of the moral superiority of the small powers, but the others in London began to view the experience of the immediate past and Norway's role in the future in a different light. It was decided by the Cabinet that a new course in foreign policy would have to be charted, and the burden of navigation was turned over to Trygve Lie.[16]

Thus a new leadership possessing new views and making different judgments both with regard to ends and means in foreign policy took command. Obviously, the Norwegian Foreign Office was primarily concerned with doing its part as a member of the United Nations in prosecuting the war. On the other hand, the Norwegian foreign policy leadership spent a great deal of time, energy, and talent thinking about and planning for Norwegian participation in the postwar world to which all looked.[17] Thus an analysis of the verbal manifestations of this process, as well as Norwegian diplomatic activity during the course of the war is revealing of the new intellectual basis and the emerging assumptions of the Norwegian foreign policy elite. In this regard attention will be drawn to (1) the general enunciations of policy and aims by the Foreign Minister, the King, and other members of the government in London, (2) Norwegian relations with, and views toward, Fenno-Scandinavia, (3) Norwegian relations with the U.S.S.R., and (4) Norwegian policy toward the evolving United Nations Organization.

The emergence of new concepts.—In a broadcast to the Norwegian people on the evening of December 15, 1940, over the BBC, Lie stated in general terms the revolutionary "new look" in Norwegian foreign policy thinking. Lie indicated that Norway would co-operate closely with "other free nations" in order to realize the liberation of Norway. The Acting Foreign Minister, however, did not limit himself to a discussion only of immediate war aims; he looked to the future and attempted to identify Norway's place in it. He spoke of co-operation with other Nordic peoples, but rejected any ideas of limiting Norwegian participation within the confines of Northern Europe.

Something more than a purely Nordic unity is, however, now needed. Cooperation, both *political* and economic, with all free nations is necessary—not only to rebuild all that has been destroyed, but to create security and prosperity in the future. This is an important and difficult task. It has been tried before without success. The League of Nations was such an effort. It was based on a great and promising idea, but it failed.[18]

The Acting Foreign Minister indicated that Norway would seek a broad-based relationship with other countries for the duration of the war and after; he rejected outright the idea of Norwegian participation in a Continental bloc, emphasizing the fact that Norway is a "seafaring nation, an old Atlantic people." Thus if Norden was too small a base for postwar Norwegian economic and security policy, so was Continental Europe. He emphasized that Norway must seek closer ties to the West "to whom we from old are connected by natural economic ties," because, he said, "our prosperity is entirely dependent on this." Lie also emphasized the ideological as well as the economic attraction of the West when he stated that "The nations to whom we have been the most firmly bound economically are peoples with the same traditions of freedom as ourselves." In particular he mentioned specifically the need for closer ties with the United Kingdom and the United States.

Lie also spoke of the need for political ties to the West in the postwar years, saying,

This is a mighty alliance . . . and it is a world which at the same time is forming the basis for a relationship which must and shall endure after the war; a political cooperation which will secure our national freedom, protect us against attacking tyrants, and which economically establishes social security and prevents financial crises from destroying economic life and stopping social development.[19]

Furthermore, Lie suggested that a secure future for Norway required Norwegian involvement in the war against Germany in order to acquire a position to exercise influence in the postwar world. He closed his address to the Norwegian people with a statement which presaged things to come (and which sounded strange from the lips of a Norwegian Foreign Minister):

Our future is not being shaped by our wishes and plans but our active share in the war to liberate Europe. We used to take our independence for granted. Now we have learnt that we cannot have it for nothing, and that we must be prepared to defend it. If we want to be given influence in the new world after the war, we must do our duty and shoulder our share in this war as far as our strength goes.[20]

That this speech represented a radical departure from traditional Norwegian foreign policy can hardly be denied. While Lie urged those at home to fight for the liberation of the country, he also informed them that the end had come to the years of isolation in the foreign policy of their country. That political collaboration with great powers was no longer taboo was clear; indeed, such collaboration was now viewed as instrumental in the economic well-being and political security of the nation. Perhaps most important however, is the thrust of the entire speech, a formulation which clearly revealed that the leading Norwegian policy-maker was acting on the basis of calculations about the nature of the political universe in which he found himself rather than on the basis of *a priori* assumptions and normative assertions. This is clearly revealed in Lie's analysis of the economic and security potentialities of Scandinavia, in his assertion that Norway's future was not shaped by "wishes" alone, and in the total absence of any great power–small power argumentation (with its attendant moral trappings). In a very real way, Lie was acting on the basis of unobscured internationalist assumptions, viz., the only foundation for economic stability and progress and political security was broad-based international cooperation. Lie's first major public statement from his new position in the Foreign Office reveals in a paradoxical and ironic fashion the rudimentary internationalism of his predecessor.

The significance of this major address by the Norwegian Foreign Minister was not missed by those in London. The day following the speech a lead editorial in the *Times* of London observed that "the present war has virtually destroyed . . . the reality of neutral status," and that Norway was the first government to recognize this. The *Times* also commented on Lie's recognition that "Scandinavian unity and Scandinavian neutrality which had seemed an adequate bulwark in the past were no longer enough," and the Foreign Minister's commitment to cooperation beyond the immediate tasks imposed by the war. In short, the *Times* inferred from the speech (and not without reason) a statement to the Norwegian people signifying a clear-cut break with the past.[21]

Parenthetically, it should be noted that the new line taken by the Foreign Minister was not without its opponents. It was opposed, first, by a hard-core group of Norwegians in London and Stockholm who continued to look to a postwar Norwegian neutrality,[22] and second, from the Central European bloc of nations headed by Poland. The basis of opposition of the latter was the fear that a grouping of nations around the Atlantic basin would place them outside the area of its interests and thus would not serve the security needs of the Central European countries. Lie's explicit rejection of a Norwegian inclusion in a Central European bloc especially troubled the Poles: above all they feared the absence of a Western commitment in Central Europe which would leave them to the designs of the Germans.[23]

The new Foreign Minister had only just begun, and by the beginning of 1941 he was firmly in the saddle in the Foreign Office when Koht resigned. A concrete manifestation of Lie's new foreign policy was seen in the spring when he signed a military agreement with the British containing an important political clause.[24] Thus, for the first time in modern history Norway had entered into a political and military alliance with another nation, and a great power at that.[25]

The next major statement of Norwegian foreign policy came in the fall of 1941 in the form of an article by the Foreign Minister in the London *Times*.[26] Lie began his article, entitled "A Community of Nations," with the statement that "the Norwegian people have been convinced that the policy of neutrality is bankrupt." Lie stated that Norway had no frontier problems nor territorial ambitions, yet he proceeded to restate a conviction expressed in his first major statement: "Intimate international cooperation will be needed after the war in the political, military, and economic fields." He indicated that Norway intended to participate, and then addressed himself to a consideration of the direction of and conditions for Norwegian co-operation in the postwar world.

As an Atlantic people we want above all a strong organized collaboration between the two great Atlantic Powers: the British Empire and the United States. This is our primary concern and the very condition of our participation in any international order in Europe.[27]

Then, in what is undoubtedly the generic conceptualization of what became the basis of Norwegian foreign policy in the early postwar period, Lie stated that the prerequisite to any extended international co-operation would depend on "an amicable relationship between the British Empire, the United States, the Soviet Union, and China."[28] He then observed, again breaking with the norms of Norwegian foreign ministers, that international co-operation must beget "practical results."

Regarding future security arrangements, Lie made it clear that here too he anticipated collaboration.

As far as the small states are concerned these duties should be primarily regional. For Norway, it seems natural to think of the defense of the Atlantic and strongly to emphasize our desire to see the US participating in this task. Military and political questions being closely connected we must also work together in the political tasks which will have to be tackled after the war. . . .[29]

The Foreign Minister also made oblique reference to the other Scandinavian states in this article when he stated that unlike the other Northern countries, whose ideological and strategic considerations are often in conflict, Norway's strategic, economic, and ideological interests "all point in the same direction." He said that he hoped that "the relations of good neighborliness" could be maintained after the war; beyond that, however, he did not go.

The only new political assertion in this article was the Foreign Minister's reference to the long period of friendly relations between the Soviet Union and Norway and his hope that these would continue; otherwise, the article is an elaboration, an affirmation and expansion of his earlier thinking: Norway was finished with neutrality and looked to collaboration with the great powers in the postwar period; Scandinavian relations were important, but their strategic problems were different and Scandinavia as an economic unit was too restricted; security could be realized only through the instrument of an international organization, the basis of which would have to be an amicable relationship among the great powers; and finally, Norwegian leaders postulated the Atlantic region, including the U.S. and Great Britain, as the primary basis of their collaborative efforts.

By this time, the Foreign Minister's position in the Foreign Office was unassailable; opposition to his new policy had withered; close collaboration with the British government had been effected; and all the major governments, including the U.S.[30] and the U.S.S.R.,[31] now recognized the Norwegian government in London, a government which was financially independent, playing a major role in the Allied war effort, and planning for an active participation in the postwar period. The subsequent development of Norwegian foreign policy can be usefully observed by examining her relations with Sweden.

Norway's relations with Norden in World War II.—As a political entity neither Norden nor Scandinavia existed during World War II, much unlike the experience of Scandinavia in World War I. Denmark, of course, was occupied by the Germans, and the Danish government was forced by the Germans to break off relations with the Norwegian government in London. Although unofficial relations between the two countries existed, official communication was of little significance. Iceland, soon after the German invasion of Denmark, declared her independence from Denmark, but was for all practical purposes an occupied country during the course of the war [32] and Norwegian-Icelandic contacts were of little consequence. Finland was unfortunate enough to have fought two wars with the Russians, losing both of them, and was thus hardly in a position to play an important role in wartime policy development.[33]

Thus, Norwegian relations with Norden during World War II were largely limited to her relations with Sweden. Norwegian-Swedish relations were often strained during the course of the war, and the issues of conflict were both concrete and symbolic. The major concrete issues involved the refusal of the

Swedish government to accept a new Norwegian Ambassador when the Norwegian Minister in Stockholm died in the fall of 1940 [34] and Sweden's policies toward the Germans, the most significant being the Swedish-German "leave transit agreements" [35] and the "horseshoe traffic" [36] arrangements, both of which were concluded in July of 1940. Norway forwarded numerous protests to the Swedes, and the Swedes, in reply, often indicated duress and the limitations of their neutrality policy.[37] While the Norwegians were undoubtedly distressed with the Swedish government's action in these and other matters, the government was also of the opinion that Sweden's continued neutrality was essential to Norwegian interests, and that the Allies must refrain from any action which might tend to compromise Swedish neutrality. This view was prompted not only by a concern for the resistance movement in Norway but was also an expression of sensitivity (prior to German invasion of the Soviet Union) for Soviet views of a great power foothold in the North, a sensitivity often expressed by former Foreign Minister Koht [38] and not unrecognized by Lie.

In addition, fundamental disagreement emerged between Sweden and Norway regarding the symbolic issue of the nature of postwar relationships in the North. As mentioned previously, the Poles were concerned about the emerging Atlantic orientation of the Norwegian government in London, and they were vigorously lobbying their plans for European regional pacts following the conclusion of hostilities. Many Swedes were favorably disposed toward the plans of the Poles, which would have included a northern defense arrangement. As early as 1941 former Swedish Foreign Minister Sandler published a booklet in which he advocated a northern confederation with common military, economic, and foreign policies; and in 1943 Stockholm's Governor-General Thorsten Nothin argued in support of a neutral postwar northern union. At the same time, Swedish Defense Minister Sköld also spoke of the utility of a Northern defense arrangement, but he too maintained that it would have to be one of armed neutrality. He asserted that those who wanted Sweden to join in with the great powers were only insuring that the North would be involved in any future war.[39] Thus future Nordic co-operation was a topic of lively discussion in Sweden as well as in London. Many projects were discussed, and one went so far as to propose a federation with the Swedish city of Drottningholm as the capital.[40]

During 1942 these discussions in Sweden particularly irritated the Norwegians: the Allies were having great difficulties and the Norwegians were of the opinion that it was, at the least, tactless of the Swedes to sustain discussion of such a delicate issue.[41] Complicating matters was a statement by a member of the British government[42] in June of 1942, expressing publicly the advantages of a Nordic alliance as an effective means of controlling the entrance to the Baltic. In short, these views, which conveniently corresponded to those advocated by the Poles, were sharply attacked by the Norwegian government in London.[43] The Norwegians continued to resist all ideas and commitments that would tie Norway closely either to the Continent or to her Northern neighbors in the postwar period. The Government in London continued to insist that Norway was an "Atlantic nation," and it persisted in its so-called Atlantic policy.

It is against this immediate background and the fundamental reorientation of Norwegian policy that had occurred since November, 1940, that the Foreign Office in the summer of 1942 circulated a document entitled *The Main Principles of Norwegian Foreign Policy*.

This document, first of all, denounced neutrality as a sound basis for Norwegian foreign policy, and declared that only universal co-operation with other nations would insure peace in the postwar world. The document indicated that the creation of a new League was desirable and that Norwegian interests were best served by co-operation with the Atlantic powers. The document did not reject outright intra-Scandinavian co-operation, but it limited it largely to the economic, social, and cultural fields, pointing out that economic co-operation among the Scandinavian countries had always been weak and their economies were competitive, not complementary.[44] The document also affirmed earlier Norwegian rejection of any close association with the

European continent, especially in the area of military security, pointing out once again that strategic considerations required Norway in the future to secure co-operation with the Atlantic powers in order to protect her long and vulnerable coast line. Finally, it stated the desirability of a regional Atlantic defense arrangement within the framework of a multifunctional world organization.

Thus *The Main Principles* was a general recapitulation and reaffirmation of the various policy statements that had been made by the government since Trygve Lie had assumed the top job in the Foreign Office. Its basic assumption was that the strategic position of Norway was fundamentally different (i.e., more vulnerable) from that of the other Nordic countries, and that Norway's economic problems could not be solved within a Scandinavian framework; on the contrary, in both cases, Norway's future, taking into consideration both economic and strategic factors, lay with sustained ties to the Atlantic countries.[45]

The Main Principles was never made public, but it was approved by the government in London and later sent to the home-front leadership, whereupon it received comment by Halvard Lange [46] and others. The home-front leadership also emphasized the need for a world-embracing organization, but it indicated less enthusiasm for the regional plans. In general, the home front, having acquired a different perspective in the war, was somewhat more favorably disposed toward closer relations with Sweden after the war, and it was more skeptical of commitments to the great powers.[47]

In the summer of 1943, one year after the writing of *The Main Principles* the government sent out a note to all of its legations for the purpose of clarifying its policy toward Sweden. The note pointed out that while Norway wished good relations with Sweden after the war, it was not going to sever its close connections with the Allies. The note quoted Foreign Minister Lie's speech of January 1, 1943, in which he said,

We believe in Nordic cooperation, but we are opposed to Nordic isolation. The Nordic countries' freedom is dependent on the United Nations victory and we will not in the future be able to exist as self-sufficient nations if we do not seek cooperation with other free people.[48]

The note further pointed out that Norway would be compelled to co-operate with the Allies after the war, both with respect to the peace negotiations and with respect to its future security. "The Norwegian Government cannot after the war break with the United Nations and isolate itself in a neutral Nordic bloc." The note did not preclude future agreements between Norway and the other Nordic countries, but it pointed out that "such agreements must be concluded within the framework of cooperation among the United Nations," in this context referring to the Allies. The government also felt that the other Nordic countries would join the organization that would be established at the conclusion of the hostilities, and it rejected, pointedly, any form of co-operation among the Nordic countries except that based on the continued sovereignty of each of the states. The note said,

The Government is therefore not a party to thought about a union of states. And it is believed that proposals concerning the establishment of a new common Nordic constitutional organ will only interfere with Nordic cooperation in the future.

The note added,

We have the impression that those in responsible positions in Sweden are also gradually beginning to understand this.[49]

Thus, the Norwegian government, without equivocation, expressed its position regarding its future political orientation. An institutionalized constitutional arrangement with the Nordic countries was rejected outright, while the government left the door open for the expansion of Nordic co-operation in the cultural and social fields. Although the government refrained from making a commitment to a political entity following the war, it likewise refused to preclude Norwegian inclusion in future agreements with the great powers.

Of relevance at this point is an article which appeared in the United States in the fall of 1943 written by Edvard Hambro, the son of the previously mentioned influential C. J. Hambro.[50] Hambro gave expression to the new foreign policy conceptualizations that have been examined above; in addition, however, he wrote of the need for a new League following the war and of Norway's participation in it. He said the Norwegians, advocating universality, "do not mean that sub-groups within the larger framework cannot be both possible and desirable." Hambro added,

Certain problems can in fact be settled well and effectively by groups of states, if these groups are the natural result of practical need and entirely loyal to the aims of the universal organization.[51]

Thus, seeming to open the door to a Scandinavian arrangement, he quickly shut it, arguing that "the Scandinavian situation is not . . . as simple as it was supposed to be before the war started." He pointed out that Norway was the only state that was actively participating in the cause of the Allies, since Iceland was essentially an occupied country, Finland was in the camp of the enemy, Denmark was not fighting the Germans, and Sweden was successfully remaining neutral, notwithstanding that "she has violated the classical laws of neutrality and given the Germans certain concessions in order to keep the peace." Furthermore, in looking to the future Hambro explicitly ruled out institutionalized co-operation among the Scandinavian countries as the answer to the problems that Norway would face:

There has been a strong revival of Scandinavian sentiment . . . in Sweden during the war. There are circles who talk about a "Nordic Defense League," and others who talk even more strongly of a "United States of the North"—very often with an open or hidden presumption of Swedish leadership. There are even Swedes who talk openly of leading Norwegian foreign policy. The answer to the speculations is, first of all, that the Norwegians like the Swedes, but do not wish to be united with them.[52]

Hambro did not discount the utility of Scandinavian collaboration, and he pointed out that the Norwegians continued to be rather sentimental about the North. He quickly added, however, that

> the post-war world will have very little use for sentimentality; and the Norwegians will not forget that they have fought this war and fought it with the Allies. Norway belongs with them.[53]

Collaboration on the cultural level with the other Nordic countries was to be expected, but Hambro wrote that political priorities would be different than they had been prior to the war,

> . . . politically the order of importance for Norway's role must be a (1) United Nations state, (2) Maritime state, (3) Atlantic state, (4) North sea state, and (5) Scandinavian state.[54]

His use of the term "United Nations state" is probably with reference to a future international organization rather than to the Allies, for later he writes that if the United Nations "should not become a reality after the war" then Norway would have to look for "other solutions," of which he cited two: an Anglo-Saxon bloc or a Scandinavian bloc.

Thus Hambro expressed the dominant attitudes that provided the intellectual basis of current thinking in London regarding the main course for Norway to follow at the war's end. Norway would not turn her back on Scandinavia, but at the same time the government did not feel that a Scandinavian bloc could offer satisfactory solutions to the major political, economic, and security problems that would face the country in the postwar period.

Norwegian-Soviet relations.—Norwegian-Soviet relations,[55] unlike Swedish-Soviet relations, have generally been good. There has long existed in Norway an appreciation of Soviet interests in the North and in the area surrounding the Baltic. Former Foreign Minister Koht was always sensitive to the Soviet view in world politics, and his belief, often expressed, that the U.S.S.R. had a vital interest in preventing a great power foothold in the North formed a major dimension of his thinking about Norwegian foreign policy.[56] The view expressed by the Norwegian Minister in Moscow during the period of the Winter War, when Sweden and Norway were aiding the Finns, indicates the sympathy of the Norwegians for Soviet interests.

> The Scandinavian countries erased the dividing line which previously existed between them and Finland, and brought upon themselves the ill-will and suspicion of the Soviet Union and in this way urged Finland to pursue a policy which is leading it to disaster. The results for the Scandinavian states themselves may be very serious.[57]

In other words, Finland, as a border state of the Soviet Union, was susceptible to special influence and should be left to solve its own problems; the Scandinavians should respect Soviet views and should take no action that would put themselves in the same political orbit as Finland.

The Norwegians continued to be cognizant of Soviet interests after arriving in London. Even before the Soviets entered the war as an Allied power, the Norwegians cautioned the Allies not to take any action against Sweden which might force her to choose sides, for regardless of what choice she made, it was bound to be undesirable from the Soviet viewpoint.[58] The Soviet interest in Sweden's neutrality was not missed by the Norwegians.

Two concrete issues did develop during the course of the war, however. One involved alleged Soviet desires for port facilities in northern Norway, and the other was concerned with the Svalbard archipelago. Throughout the war, rumors, mentioned above in connection with Poland, abounded in London regarding Soviet intentions in north Norway. The government recognized that they were undoubtedly inflated and politically motivated, but in any case, the Norwegian bargaining position was weak, especially since the government realized, as the war wore on, that it was likely that Russian troops would be involved in the liberation of Norway. Finally the Norwegian government attempted, and succeeded in, coming to an explicit agreement with the Soviet government regarding its role in and after the liberation. This agreement, however, did not seem to reduce the frequency of alleged Soviet intentions in north Norway.

When Foreign Minister Lie visited Washington in 1943, the U.S. President informed him of Soviet desires for the use of Norwegian port and rail facilities, indicating that he was hopeful of reaching a compromise solution, which might, for example, involve making Narvik an internationally-administered port. Thus, for the first time there was official confirmation of Soviet interest in Norwegian port facilities. Lie was opposed to the suggestions made by the President and informed him that only the Norwegian people could make such a decision. The issue was never pressed further by the President, however, and the Soviet government failed to make its interests known directly to the Norwegians; thus the matter never reached crisis proportions.[59]

Later, in 1944, a question was raised directly by the Soviet government concerning Svalbard. The Russians desired a modification of the Treaty of 1920 that had placed Svalbard under Norwegian jurisdiction.[60] The Soviet view was that the Soviet Union had not been in a position in 1920 to protect its interests in this vital area of the world, and consequently the Treaty ought to be modified.[61]

The Norwegians, surprised by the raising of the issue, were in a very poor bargaining position vis-à-vis the Soviet Union at this time: Norway was still occupied by German troops with the exception of those parts in the North which had already been liberated by the Russians. Furthermore, the Norwegians were very much dependent on the good will of all their allies, and especially the Soviets, in order to bring about the hasty liberation of the entire country. Thus, the Norwegians trod lightly: they recognized the legitimacy of Soviet strategic concern for the northern area, if not the legitimacy of Soviet claims; they did not want to precipitate a crisis with the Soviet Union. The government responded by appointing a blue-ribbon committee[62] to study the problem and, in effect, bought time. The matter was raised on several occasions in succeeding years, but the question of revising the Treaty of 1920 was never pressed to any conclusion by the Soviet Union (although there were times in the postwar period when Soviet intentions were dangerously hazy), and the Soviets eventually dropped the Svalbard matter. The Norwegian government thus succeeded in postponing indefinitely a decision in a situation where its bargaining position was inherently weak and further complicated by the high priority it placed on continued good relations with the U.S.S.R. During the course of the discussion of the issue, until 1947 when it was finally dropped by the Soviets, it became clear that the primary Soviet concern was strategic, and reciprocal Norwegian concern for Soviet strategic interests was clearly revealed.[63]

Norway and the United Nations Organization.—That Norway was anticipating the postwar organization of the international community became clear with Lie's first major address in December, 1940, and continued to be stated as the war years drew to a close. *The Main Principles* had referred to the need for a comprehensive international organization as had Hambro's article in the fall of 1943. In the summer of 1944 King Haakon delivered a speech to the Foreign Press Association in London where he recounted the contributions the small powers had made to the defeat of Germany and where he repeated that international collaboration, and not neutrality, would be the only hope for national security in the postwar world. He again revealed the new attitude of the Norwegians toward the role of the great powers in the postwar world:

. . . the small states must be consulted. We must participate in the actual making of decisions, and not be presented only with accomplished facts. We do not ask for the small states the right to veto decisions or to paralyze the international organization. We are prepared to let the great powers play the leading role they have the right to play.[64]

The King postulated a major role for an international organization in future Norwegian foreign and security policy and revealed the degree to which distrust of the great powers no longer occupied a central position in Norwegian official thinking.

The Foreign Minister re-emphasized these and other major points in a broadcast in January, 1944, to the Norwegian people reflecting the new concepts that now prevailed in the Foreign Office in London. He cited again the need for collaboration with the democratic states around the North Atlantic basin and the importance of continued good relations among the great powers.

Norway's interests would best be served by an agreement embracing the lands around the North Atlantic, presupposing that this would be subordinate to an international organization, and accompanied by an extension of our good relations with the Soviet Union. . . . The starting point must be the United Nations. . . . Mutual trust and cooperation among the Big Four is the first prerequisite of lasting peace.[65]

Thus, when the four sponsoring powers of the inchoate United Nations Organization met in San Francisco in April of 1945, the new principles and priorities in Norwegian foreign policy were revealed in bold relief in a concrete situation.

The Dumbarton Oaks proposals, which were presented as the working papers for the conference, contained provisions for a great power veto in the Security Council of the new organization, the organ that was to be responsible for the maintenance of international peace and security. The Norwegian government had already declared on several different occasions during the war that Norway's security could be founded only on a comprehensive world organization. And now, with the chips on the table, Norway was willing to give that organization the freedom of action necessary to maintain peace and meet the threats to the peace. This new policy comprehended a fundamentally revised view of the role of the great powers, a view succinctly revealed by the Foreign Minister:

The great powers will have to shoulder the burden of providing the military and material means for maintaining the peace, and we are prepared to grant them an international status corresponding to their responsibility.[66]

Of course, the two important sections that gave the great powers the "international status corresponding to their responsibility" was the protection (to all) granted under the veto system, contained in Chapter V of the Charter and the power granted to the Security Council to undertake appropriate preventive or enforcement action in the name of the United Nations. The endorsement of such a radical proposal by a Norwegian Foreign Minister six years previously would have been unthinkable. Commenting on the Dumbarton Oaks proposals the Norwegian Royal Commission stated,

In the Dumbarton Oaks proposals we face a novel conception. They aim at creating an international institution of action instead of an organization that is primarily deliberative. They try to create international security through an international concentration of power . . . [because freedom of action is restricted the Commission is faced with the question]: Is the security offered worth the sacrifice one is asked to make? Can a small state risk placing its destiny in the hands of the proposed Security Council? We are tempted to reply: It cannot risk not to do so.[67]

The Commission then opined that World War II proved that "under the technical conditions of our time no state is alone capable of defending itself against an aggressive power." The Commission also noted that the proposals had the support of the great powers and argued that this was significant because "experience has shown that no political organization can fulfill its tasks satisfactorily without including them among its members."

The Norwegian Commission then turned to the question of security for Norway and suggested that only three alternatives existed. Norway could (1) follow an independent course in world affairs: go it alone; (2) work for a weaker form of international organization, such as the League represented, and still retain freedom of action; or (3) support the Dumbarton Oaks proposals and the kind of international organization and collaboration they represented. The Commission concluded its analysis with the opinion that only a strong international organization "can lead the small states to any hope of security." [68]

Thus, Norway was placing all of its "security eggs" in one basket, the United Nations. This was the policy Trygve Lie had been pursuing since the Foreign Office came under his leadership, and Norwegian support for the veto specifically and the concept of the Security Council generally only underscored the successful culmination of that policy in a concrete situation. It represented a fundamental change not only in the image of the great powers, but also in the purpose of Norwegian foreign policy; for under the veto system in the United Nations, and with the power of the Security Council to maintain peace and security, a state whose fundamental concern was for freedom of action could not support the proposals nor would it desire great power unity. Freedom of action, which previously had been a hallmark of Norwegian foreign policy, would be possible under the UN system only if great power disunity prevailed. On the other hand, a state which looked to the new international organization as the basis of its security policy would desire amicable relations among the great powers, since the utility of the security system was contingent on the ability of the great powers to concert their actions. [69] Thus, Norway's efforts to lubricate great power relationships and mitigate their differences revealed her interest in the UN as a security instrument.

1. It is interesting to note that the German invasion of Denmark and Norway was the first combined air-sea-land operation in military history.

2. The Germans simultaneously invaded Denmark and gained control of the country within a few hours. The Danes, their government, and their King accepted the German terms, and Danish resistance was not substantial until 1943. Sweden was determined to remain neutral, and this determination was conveyed to Hitler in a message from King Gustav; Hitler, in reply, affirmed his determination to respect Swedish neutrality. Thus, the concerted policies of the Scandinavians were at their end: Sweden was neutral, Denmark had capitulated, and Norway was at war with Germany. (In fact, Norway held out against the Germans for 63 days, longer than any other nation on the western European mainland). See Rowland Kenney, *The Northern Tangle* (London: J. M. Dent, 1946), pp. 131, 156–77, 180–84.

3. The original text of the ultimatum along with an English abridgment can be found in Halvdan Koht, *Norway Neutral and Invaded* (London: Hutchinson, 1941), pp. 197–209; for an account of the crucial and exemplary role played by the King during the crisis see Maurice Michael, *Haakon, King of Norway* (New York: Macmillan, 1958), especially pp. 154–55.

4. The Germans were hopeful of establishing a "model protectorate" in Norway similar to that established in Denmark. The Germans maintained that their occupation of the country was a pre-emptive and not an aggressive act and was designed only to deny Norway to the Allies and not to employ Norwegian territory as bases of operation against the Allies. For an enlightened discussion of this point in a broader context see Jens A. Christopherson, "The Nordic Countries and the European Balance of Power," *Cooperation and Conflict*, I (1965), 46–50. For an account of the invasion, the reaction of the government, the establishment of the Quisling regime, and the underground movement, see Kenney, *op. cit.*, pp. 109–49; for an account of British intentions see Koht, *op. cit.*, pp. 47–50. For a brief description of the domestic situation see Chr. A. R. Christiansen, *Norway and World War Two* (Washington: Norwegian Information Service, 1961), pp. 1–12. On British intentions from their side see Winston S. Churchill, *The Second World War* (*The Gathering Storm*, I [London: Cassel, 1948]), pp. 490–92.

5. The circumstances surrounding the government's decision to depart the country on June 7, 1940, are discussed in C. J. Hambro, *I Saw It Happen in Norway* (New York: Appleton-Century, 1940), especially pp. 113–20.

6. See *Instilling fra undersøkelses Kommisjonen av 1945* (Oslo: Aschehoug, 1947), I, 114; and Hambro, *op. cit.*, pp. 28–29.

7. Reference here is to Article Eleven of the Norwegian Constitution. For a discussion of other constitutional problems involved in carrying on the war see Hambro, *op. cit.*, pp. 13–14, 28–31, 182–94.

8. Trygve Lie, *Med England i Ildlinjen* (Oslo: Tiden, 1956), pp. 115.

9. British, French, and Polish troops were landed in Norway, inadequately equipped and unfamiliar with the terrain, only to be withdrawn due to the deterioration of the Allied position on the Continent. See Hambro, *op. cit.*, pp. 80–81; and Kenney, *op. cit.*, pp. 122–27.

10. The most important factor in the financial independence of the government was income accruing from its continued control over the merchant marine, which was immediately put at the disposal of the Allied war effort. Its strategic importance can be seen in that in excess of 30 per cent of British oil requirements were carried in Norwegian bottoms for the duration of the war. British MP Philip Noel-Baker said in April, 1942, that "Norwegian tankers are to the battle of the Atlantic what the Spitfires were to the Battle of Britain." For details see Øyvind Lorentzen, *Norway, Norwegian Shipping, and the War* (New York: Oxford University Press, 1942) pp. 21–25; Kenney, *op. cit.*, pp. 150–51, 233; for a very interesting account of the problems encountered in maintaining control over the fleet during the chaotic period following the invasion and the establishment of the Norwegian Shipping and Trade Mission ("Nortraship") in London see Koht, *op. cit.*, pp. 177–82.

11. Koht, however, largely for personal reasons, was not well-received by many members of the British government and there was a noticeable absence of contact between him and his peers in the host country. See Lie, *op. cit.*, p. 99.

12. Reference here is to Arnold Raestad, Wilhelm Keilhau, Arne Ording, Jacob Worm-Müller, and C. J. Hambro.

13. See *Instilling fra undersøkelses Kommisjonen av 1945*, II, 40; and Lie, *op. cit.*, p. 102.

14. *Instilling fra undersøkelses Kommisjonen av 1945*, II, 40–41.

15. *Ibid.*, p. 41.

16. Koht was given a "leave of absence" and Trygve Lie immediately became Acting Foreign Minister on November 21, 1940. Koht later resigned and Lie became the Foreign Minister of the Labor government in London in February of 1941. Lie formerly had served as Minister of Supply and was respected as a competent and hard-working administrator, although he had little experience in foreign affairs. See Erik J. Friis, "Trygve Lie," *American Scandinavian Review*, XXXVI (March, 1948), 11–16.

17. Arne Ording, "Norsk utenrikspolitikk under krigen," in Sverre Steen (ed.), *Norges Krig 1940–45* (Oslo: Gyldendal, 1948), II, 229–30. The intellectual leadership of the Norwegian foreign policy community in London was provided by Arnold Raestad. The core of his ideas is found in a posthumous publication of Raestad's, *Europe and the Atlantic World* (Oslo: Aschehoug, 1958), written during the war and in numerous articles in wartime editions of the *Norseman*. The author is indebted to Professor H. P. Krosby of the University of Wisconsin for calling attention to Raestad's wartime role.

18. *Times* (London), December 16, 1940. (Italics added.) Reprinted by permission of the *Times*.

19. *Ibid.*

20. *Ibid.*

21. "The Small Nations," *Times* (London), December 16, 1940.

22. The opposition in London gathered around Koht and those in Stockholm looked to former Liberal Prime Minister Mowinckel and another prominent Norwegian, Frihagen. The influence of the Stockholm group was largely shattered by the summer of 1941; Koht's influence waned; and Lie was in firm control.

23. See Trygve Lie, *Hjemover* (Oslo: Tiden, 1958), p. 56. The Poles made numerous attempts to discourage the new Atlantic orientation of Norwegian foreign policy and attempted to pull Norway "back into Europe." The Poles were responsible for rumors about Russian designs in northern Norway; and they attempted to enlist Swedish support for their cause favoring regional European defense arrangements, including one for Europe's northern tier under Swedish leadership. These and other activities by the Poles caused problems in London, but, as will be seen, the Norwegian position was not altered.

24. Lie, *Med England i Ildlinjen*, p. 147. The Military Agreement with Great Britain was signed on May 28, 1941.

25. Clark Choffy, "The Diplomacy of Norway, 1939–1945" (unpublished Ph.D. dissertation, American University, Washington, D.C., 1960), p. 197.

26. Trygve Lie, "A Community of Nations," *Times* (London), November 14, 1941, p. 5. Lie's major emphasis in this article was with postwar economic problems; that which follows is an analysis only of his politically relevant assertions.

27. *Ibid.* This, coupled with Lie's earlier statement of December, 1940, reveals the so-called Norwegian Atlantic policy, which is, according to some observers, the product of the thinking of Dr. Arnold Raestad, a long-time opponent of neutrality. See Nils Ørvik, *Trends in Norwegian Foreign Policy* (Oslo: Norwegian Institute of International Affairs, 1962), p. 12; Wilhelm Keilhau, "Norway and the Atlantic Pact," *Norseman,* VII (March–April, 1949), 80. (Raestad served as the Governor of the Bank of Norway in London during the war.)

28. Lie, "A Community of Nations," p. 5. In the same context Lie stated, "We have all discussed the reasons why the League of Nations did not succeed . . . It would have been possible to use the League machinery against Italian and German aggression if the leading powers in the League had seriously wanted to do so. Countries adopted, however, a short-sighted policy of self-interest, and in an atmosphere of pacific public opinion nobody was willing to run any risks."

29. *Ibid.*

30. The United States, in line with its policy of the non-recognition of governments established by force, agreed on September 18, 1940, to recognize the Norwegian government-in-exile. See Cordell Hull, *The Memoirs of Cordell Hull* (New York: Macmillan, 1948), II, 751–53.

31. The Soviet Union had severed relations with Norway on May 8, 1941, undoubtedly as a consequence of the Nazi-Soviet pact of 1939. The Norwegians assumed duress and did not protest the break. Following the German attack on the Soviet Union on June 22, 1941, Norway and the U.S.S.R. resumed diplomatic relations on August 8, 1941. See Lie, *Med England i Ildlinjen,* p. 188.

32. Iceland gained her independence first in 1918 through the instrument of the Icelandic-Danish Union Act, which stipulated that Denmark would be entrusted with safeguarding Iceland's foreign affairs. On April 10, 1940, the day following the German invasion of Denmark, Iceland declared that she had assumed full sovereignty over her foreign affairs. Early in May of 1944 the final step was taken to sever the relationship with Denmark, and on June 17, 1944, the Icelandic Republic was formally inaugurated. See Gudmundur I. Gudmundsson, "The Foreign Policy of Iceland," *The American Scandinavian Review,* LIII (Summer, 1965), 125–26; Kenney, *op. cit.,* pp. 177–78; and Lie, *Med England i Ildlinjen,* p. 169. Iceland declared herself a "permanent neutral" in 1918, but following the invasion of Denmark, the British, and later (in July, 1941) the Americans engaged in a "friendly occupation" of the country for the duration of the war.

33. During the first Finnish conflict with the U.S.S.R., the Winter War, both Sweden and Norway extended aid to the Finns and worked closely with their government. When Finland became a "co-belligerent" with Germany, however, Norway broke off relations.

34. Sweden refused to provide an *agrément* to Chargé d'Affaires Jens Bull following the death of the Norwegian Minister J. H. Wollebaek in October of 1940. Bull's many efforts to gain acceptance at the Foreign Office in Stockholm failed, on the grounds that his becoming Minister would complicate Sweden's relations with Germany. Finally in November of 1943, when Sweden could afford to act more independently of Berlin, Bull was accredited. See Det Kgl. Utenriksdepartement, *Norges Forhold til Sverige under Krigen*

1940–1945 (Oslo: Gyldendal, 1948), II, 6–7, 15, 74. (Hereinafter cited as *Norges Forhold.*)

35. The "leave transit agreements" provided for the transportation of German troops across Swedish territory in order to provide rest and rehabilitation. This was a source of provocation to the Norwegian government, especially in view of the fact that the Norwegian resistance movement was still engaged in fighting the Germans and since this arrangement obviously aided the Germans. The Norwegian view held that the Swedes were not required under laws of neutrality to make such concessions to the Germans, but the Swedish position, rather strong from the point of view of international law, was that the physical departure of the Norwegian government from Norway marked an end to the hostilities, and thus the Swedes were not working against the interests of the Norwegians in any way. See Ording, *op. cit.,* p. 222.

36. The "horseshoe traffic" arrangements involved Swedish-German agreements which permitted the Germans to overcome difficulties presented by the difficult terrain in Norway, allowing them to pass through Sweden in transit between Trondheim in central Norway and Narvik in the north.

37. Swedish Foreign Minister Sandler once said in reply: "What we can do we are doing; and when we refuse something it is because we cannot do it." *Norges Forhold,* I, 17. State Secretary Boheman once stated: "All policy of neutrality has its limitations in the possibilities which are at the disposal of the neutral state." *Norges Forhold,* I, 90–91.

38. See note from Koht addressed to British and French governments on May 19, 1940; *Norges Forhold,* I, 21–23.

39. Kenney, *op. cit.,* pp. 221–23.

40. Ording, *op. cit.,* II, 226.

41. It was suggested by some that the Swedes were hoping for a compromise peace since they had no interest in seeing either Germany or the U.S.S.R. emerge from the war with control over the Baltic, and that it was within this framework that propaganda for a Nordic Union was coming from Sweden.

42. Reference here is to Sir Stafford Cripps.

43. The expressions of Cripps, for example, were attacked in the Norwegian news organ in London, *Norsk Tidende,* where it was stated that since this view was contrary to the policy of the Norwegian government it was regretted that a member of the British government would so express himself without first contacting the Norwegian government. See Ording, *op. cit.,* II, 228.

44. This point was expressed very succinctly by a Swedish opponent of the concept of a Northern Union as a solution to the problem of security in Herbert Tingsten, *The Debate about Northern Unity,* cited in Kenney, *op. cit.,* p. 222.

45. Ording, *op. cit.,* II, 229–30.

46. Lange succeeded Lie in the Foreign Office in 1946.

47. On this point, I am indebted to Mr. Helge Groth; see also Ording, *op. cit.,* II, 229–30; and Leroy Karlstrøm, "Beginning and End of Norwegian Neutrality," *Norseman,* IX (September–October, 1951), 290.

48. Quoted in Ording, *op. cit.*, II, 230.

49. *Ibid.*, pp. 230–31.

50. Edvard Hambro, "Small States and a New League: From the Point of View of Norway," *The American Political Science Review*, XXXVII (October, 1943), 903–9. At the time the article was published Hambro was a secretary for the Norwegian Foreign Office, a job he had assumed in August of 1943. Hambro insists that the article was written only in his capacity as a private person and not to expound government policy; however at the time of writing he was in close touch with his father who, he says, influenced his thinking on these matters. Hambro, a professor, a former member of Parliament and Norwegian UN ambassador, participated in the San Francisco Conference in 1945 and then went on to work for the UN and the ICJ. (Information from personal correspondence with Mr. Hambro, April 7, 1965.)

51. *Ibid.*, p. 906.

52. *Ibid.*

53. *Ibid.*

54. *Ibid.*, p. 908.

55. Norwegian-Soviet relations in World War II were not especially conspicuous; they are treated here, however, because of the subsequent role of the Soviet Union in the formulation of Norwegian foreign policy.

56. See for example a statement by Koht in *Instilling fra Undersøkelses Kommisjonen av 1945*, pp. 40–41.

57. *Instilling fra Undersøkelses Kommisjonen av 1945*, Supplement I, p. 202; throughout the Winter War Norwegian support of Finland was much more reserved than Sweden's, and this did not go unnoticed in Moscow. See on this Egil Danielsen, *Norge-Sovjetunionen: Norges Utenrikspolitikk overfor Sovjetunionen 1917–1940* (Oslo: Universitetsforlaget, 1964), pp. 245–46.

58. *Norges Forhold*, I, 21–23.

59. Lie, *Hjemover*, pp. 85–87; and Choffy, *op. cit.*, p. 262.

60. The question was broached when Foreign Minister Lie and Justice Minister Wold were in Moscow in November, 1944, to discuss problems connected with Soviet military operations which had begun in North Norway in October, 1944. Soviet troops liberated North Norway (and in the process built up a large store of good will).

61. Molotov proposed that Bjørnøya (Bear Island) be ceded to the U.S.S.R. and that the entire archipelago be placed under a Russo-Norwegian condominium, maintaining that the question affected Soviet security as well as Russian economic interests. For a discussion of the entire episode see Trygve Mathisen, *Svalbard in the Changing Arctic* (Oslo: Gyldendal, 1954), chap. iv, pp. 46–60; and Lie, *Hjemover*.

62. The Committee consisted of H. C. Berg, C. J. Hambro, Arne Ording, and Arnold Raestad.

63. See Mathisen, *op. cit.*, pp. 52–53 for a discussion of the proposals agreed to by the Storting in an attempt to accommodate the Soviet's demands.

64. *Times* (London), June 8, 1944.

65. Cited in Kenney, *op. cit.*, p. 219.

66. T. P. Svennevig, "The Scandinavian Bloc in the United Nations and Its New Outlook," *Norseman*, XIII (May–June, 1955), 148. At San Francisco, Norway did not support the Australian proposal to do away with the veto power.

67. Quoted in Einar Løchen and Rolf N. Torgersen, *Norway's Views on Sovereignty* (Oslo: Chr. Michelsens Institutt, 1955), pp. 36–37.

68. *Ibid*. The Storting ratified the UN Charter by a unanimous vote on November 16, and it was deposited with the UN on November 27, 1945. Thus Norway and Denmark were the only two of the Nordic countries to become Charter members of the United Nations. On this see Leland M. Goodrich and Edvard Hambro, *Charter of the United Nations: Commentary and Documents* (Boston: World Peace Foundation, 1949), pp. 545–46.

69. W. E. Rappard, "The UN From a European Point of View, *Yale Law Review*, LV (1945–46), 1047; Finn Moe, "Norway and the United Nations," *Norseman*, XVI (November–December, 1958), 367 73.

CHAPTER III

The Search for Security:
Bridgebuilding in the United Nations

The strategic image at the beginning of the postwar period.—As the preceding has suggested, the German invasion demonstrated the inefficacy of neutrality, but this evaluation did not reflect itself in Norwegian foreign policy until the winter of 1940 when the leadership in the Foreign Office changed hands. The new leadership, however, came to power with a totally revised strategic image providing the basis for fundamental policy changes.

The strategic image that evolved during the course of the war was complex and comprehensive, and it seems that the most immediate cause for the total revision was the impact of the German invasion, even though that event had at the time little influence on the perceptions of the old leadership.[1]

The new policy elite continued to perceive the structure of the international system in terms of great powers and small powers; however, the affective component which had supplemented this perception prior to World War II dissolved during the course of the war. No longer were the great powers to be condemned for their "political" orientation and charged with a lack of concern for, if not intention to undermine, the rights and dignities of the small powers.

Related is the alteration of the process image. No longer a "cabal," the international system was now perceived as a "community of nations" where the great powers would necessarily play a decisive and dynamic role. The small states were a part of this international "community" and would have to refrain from obstructing the international political process and give to the great powers a status corresponding to their encompassing responsibilities. Thus power and responsibility were now perceived as linked, if not synonymous.

The process of international politics was now viewed as one greatly influenced by the great powers in consultation with the small, and the international system was perceived as an inchoate community from which isolation was impossible, requiring, on the contrary, involvement and responsibility by all, both for national security and economic stability and progress. The most significant axiom deriving from this new image was the assertion that the dilemma of national security could not be solved on a national basis. Relative to this perception was a partial rejection of the traditional liberal tenets that postulated the attainment of peace from the discussion and understanding achieved through international institutions such as arbitration and conciliation commissions. While the Norwegians continued to value processes of peaceful settlement, conflict prevention and resolution tended to be viewed in more Machiavellian terms: "the peace must be maintained with power." [2]

The action component of the strategic image was also modified. History now "proved" the bankruptcy of neutrality. Although Norway had been able to avoid war for more than a century and a quarter, it was now asserted that the successes of the past were perhaps fortuitous, and consequently the lessons of the distant past were refuted by the lessons of the immediate past. Directly linked was the revised judgment of Norway's geographic location. Norwegian policy-makers were sensitive to what they called the changing "technique" of warfare, referring primarily to the advent of strategic air power. Also they were cognizant, perhaps earlier than most, of the emergence of two new power centers, for they often spoke of the postwar political world in terms of "Britain and America on the one side and Soviet Russia on the other." Further, perhaps resulting from their experience with the problems connected with Svalbard late in the war, the Norwegians indicated an awareness of the significance for them of the emerging political pattern when coupled with the new "technique" and the resulting polar strategy.[3] In short, the Norwegians perceived their geographic location no longer as "peripheral" but rather as potentially exposed or "strategic," which, in the event of war, would provide little opportunity for a posture of non-involvement or the status of a non-belligerent. Thus a small state could no longer hope to insure unilaterally its own security nor long endure a general war.

The foregoing basic revisions of the Norwegian strategic image corresponded to a fundamental reorientation of expectations about the nature of the postwar world as far as Norway was concerned: in the future, peace would be indivisible, and security for any nation would be dependent on the ability and determination of all nations to co-operate in promoting new forms of international organization having the ability to prevent violence and to control and localize armed conflict should it nevertheless occur.

Thus is encountered a response flowing from the structure of the strategic image. Even though the traditional great power–small power stereotype had been displaced, the Norwegians indicated that the small states, limited as they were in their ability to mold the course of events in international politics, still retained influence which could be exploited. It was this final judgment coupled with the other components of the strategic image that formed the basis of the immediate postwar foreign policy of Norway.

In this regard, it should be noted that ideological preferences became more salient in Norwegian policy enunciations during the first years of the war (as compared with the immediate prewar years). Norwegian leaders spoke of "free nations" and the "Atlantic democracies." Although many of the pronouncements can be attributed to the special circumstances created by the war, the Foreign Minister in several of his early statements indicated that he was referring to the influence ideological factors would inevitably have on postwar Norwegian policy. However, ideological references became less frequent as the war continued. The German attack on the U.S.S.R. and the latter's emergent status as one of the Allies undoubtedly was influential and was reflected in a policy statement by the Foreign Minister in the fall of 1941. Most influential, however, was the evolution of the United Nations Organization, for after it became clear that a comprehensive world organization with security functions would be created, Norwegian policy enunciations tended to become more focused and specific, concentrating on concrete problems rather than on symbolic issues. It will be recalled that early in the war the Norwegians emphasized, with reference to the postwar world, (1) the need for a universal international organization, (2) the desirability of regional organization, and (3) the ideological (and economic) attraction of the Atlantic basin countries on Norway. However, as the postwar world drew nearer and as the international organization began to take concrete form, the Norwegians spoke less of regional arrangements and hardly ever in ideological terms. In other words, the establishment of an international security organization and its success became the most important single objective of Norwegian policy during the war's final years, and in this concern few expressions giving priority to ideological factors can be discerned. Thus by the end of the war, ideological factors were not noticeable in the articulations of Norwegian foreign policy.

With regard to the early assertion of the need for regional arrangements, two developments in Norwegian thinking during the war should be noted. First, the rejection by the Norwegian policy elite in London of a Norwegian tie to an isolated Scandinavian political or economic arrangement following the war continued to be affirmed throughout the course of the war, as did the unconditional rejection of Norwegian ties to a Central European bloc. In the first case the Norwegians perceived the Scandinavian area as too small to provide solutions to either economic or security problems, and an isolated European bloc was rejected outright as irrational and unthinkable. Second, and related, the Norwegians early in the war talked often of a postwar political and economic arrangement among the nations around the Atlantic basin, their so-called Atlantic policy. However, in the later war years statements referring to an Atlantic arrangement were less frequent, and when the Atlantic region was considered, it was always within the framework of, and supplementary to, the embryonic United Nations Organization.[4]

Thus, two generalizations derive from the above observations: one, the Norwegian strategic image (especially the image of process and geography) was redefined in a fundamental way and second, Norwegian policy statements, derived from the strategic image and oriented toward, and based on, predictions about the nature of the postwar world, revealed the high, indeed almost exclusive, priority attached to the establishment of an international *security* organization. In this respect, it should be noted that the Norwegian government made many symbolic and concrete commitments to the embryonic United Nations Organization even before the war was concluded, and this continuing commitment in the postwar world is what has been called the Norwegian policy of "bridgebuilding."

The policy of bridgebuilding.—The Norwegians suffered very heavy losses in World War II. More than one-half of their prewar shipping tonnage had been destroyed, the entire northern third of the country lay in waste as a result of the scorched-earth policies of the Germans, and the economy was severely undermined and weakened as a result of the economic policies of the occupation authorities.[5]

Thus in the first months following the liberation, the government was almost totally occupied with innovating and implementing a reconstruction and stabilization program.[6] These points are mentioned because most analysts of postwar Norwegian foreign policy have inferred from this preoccupation with domestic problems a "return to neutrality" (sometimes hedged with the use of the enigmatic term "quasi-neutrality") by the Norwegian foreign policy elite.[7] As the foregoing analysis would suggest, such a characterization of Norwegian foreign policy would border on gross distortion, confusing, perhaps, inactivity with calculated non-involvement. As will be demonstrated below, Norwegian foreign policy continued in the early postwar years as the policy elite indicated it would in the latter war years, and this policy can hardly be classed as neutrality, regardless of the qualifying adjective.

In the fall following the liberation [8] the Norwegians held a general election in which the Labor party secured an absolute majority in the Storting for the first time,[9] and in which the Communists won eleven seats, reflecting in part the important role they played in the home front, but reflecting also the great store of good will which existed toward the Soviet Union as a result of its major role in the liberation of north Norway.[10] The feeling toward the Communists in general and the U.S.S.R. in particular is relevant to postwar Norwegian foreign policy, for it demonstrates the absence in Norway, unlike in many other countries, of a deep-rooted fear of a Communist coup, nor was there evidence in Norway of the Russophobia which existed in many other Western nations.[11]

It should also be emphasized in this regard that Russian foreign policy during the first months of the postwar period was viewed by Norway largely in the framework of the *Soviet* search for security. While the Norwegians were aware of the Soviet desire for an outlet to the sea, they did not perceive a threat to themselves from the Soviet side,[12] and this sanguine view of Soviet intentions was reinforced in the spring of 1947 when the Soviets dropped the Svalbard issue almost as unexpectedly as they raised it in 1944.

To return to the major point, however, in the immediate postwar period the Norwegians, far from returning to a policy of neutrality, pursued without reservation a policy that was clearly predicated on, and consistent with, the evaluations and perceptions that emerged during the war. As the tensions and differences of view between the U.S. and the U.S.S.R. became manifest, the Norwegians exerted every effort to mediate and mitigate these differences and antagonisms. Trygve Lie had stated as early as 1941 that in the Norwegian view the only basis for security in the postwar world would be that founded on a comprehensive international organization and on the basis of co-operation among the great powers. Once the UN had become a reality the Norwegians resisted all attempts toward bloc-building inside the organization, especially the early attempts to set the small powers against the great powers and, later, the tendency of the great powers to separate. In a speech to the First General Assembly, Lie stated clearly that the basis of Norwegian foreign policy had not changed. He said, reflecting on the experience in the interwar period, that Norway had long believed that the only hope for peace was a world organization; therefore, Norway supported all efforts toward international collaboration, but

At the same time it was based on an earnest desire to keep out of any conflict and on the assumption that a declaration of neutrality constituted a guarantee of being kept out of the war.[13]

Lie went on to say that

The German invasions dispelled the idea that one can keep out of war by staying neutral . . . [Thus] Norway has hoped for and advocated the formation of an organization such as the United Nations.

He then stated the basis of, and reasons for, contemporary Norwegian foreign policy:

Not only will our participation in [the UN's] work be the basis of our foreign policy . . . the time has passed when the initiative rested with the small states alone. . . . The Norwegian delegation now shares the opinion that peace is one and indivisible. . . . Unless we realize this fact, no useful results can be hoped for. That is why those who really wish to further the cause of world peace . . . should not try to divide the world into separate blocs.

With reference to the great powers, the Foreign Minister said that they had greater responsibilities than the other members, and that

without confident and sincere cooperation between all the great powers, our work would utterly fail and world peace would be a fiction . . . if this first and essential condition of peace and security did not exist.

This, Lie concluded, was the reason the Norwegian government did not object to the formal and constitutional influence given to the great powers, a status which reflected political reality and corresponded to their greater responsibilities. He then went on to explain the meaning of "bridgebuilding."

> The smaller nations have a great part to play in cementing the peace. They are disinterested in many political disputes; their ambitions are cultural and economic. And so, in the opinion of the Norwegian delegation, their foreign policy should aim at making a sincere contribution to the mutual understanding and confidence of the great powers.

This, then, was the essence and rationale of the early postwar policy of "bridgebuilding." The Norwegians realized that great power agreement was a *sine qua non* for an effective United Nations; therefore, political responsibility required them to make all attempts to work for great power consensus in order to insure great power unanimity. Likewise, they opposed all actions that did not hold the promise of practical results and that might lead to the formation of great power blocs within the Organization or that might result in great power enmity. This policy within the UN was required because the security policy of Norway was based on the effectiveness and success of that Organization.

When Trygve Lie was elected the first Secretary General of the United Nations,[14] most observers interpreted the outcome as a vote of confidence in the national policy he had authored and successfully implemented, for the Norwegian government had been able to gain the trust of the Soviet Union without simultaneously forfeiting the confidence of the United States and the other Western powers. His successor in the Foreign Office, Halvard Lange,[15] reaffirmed the political goals of his predecessor.[16] Thus the basis of Norwegian security policy rested in the United Nations, and Norway continued to exert all efforts toward creating political unity among the great powers, a unity without which the UN could not function as an effective politico-security instrument. Therefore, great power co-operation was the highest priority in Norwegian foreign policy and the essential prerequisite of Norwegian security policy.

Before proceeding further with the foreign policy of Norway, it should be noted that Scandinavian co-operation, which had been largely destroyed during the war years, began anew following the conclusion of hostilities. Denmark and Norway sponsored Swedish membership in the United Nations and, following Swedish acceptance, consultations occurred regularly among the Scandinavian governments prior to General Assembly sessions, and continuous consultations took place among the delegations at the meetings.[17] The Scandinavian voting bloc at the United Nations from the beginning has been one of the most cohesive, and it is not unusual for one of the members of the bloc to act as spokesman for all.

Following the war proposals continued to be forwarded regarding the establishment of a Scandinavian customs union and favoring a Nordic defense arrangement. The Norwegian government did not respond directly to those suggestions for a defense arrangement [18] because its foreign policy, based as it was on the United Nations, not only did not require regional defense arrangements, but always opposed explicitly the establishment of regional defense alliances.[19] In an interview in January, 1946, the Foreign Minister (Lie) said that Norway did not favor a Scandinavian defense bloc, although everyone hoped for continued Scandinavian co-operation. Security today, he said, depended exclusively upon harmonious relations among the great powers.[20] However the government did publicly and officially oppose suggestions for the establishment of a Scandinavian customs union, arguing, as it did during the war, that the small market area and the non-complementary nature of the Scandinavian countries' economies, made a customs union economically irrational.[21]

Nevertheless, Scandinavian collaboration in foreign policy must be recognized as important. The Swedes continued to assert their policy of neutrality, or, as they more frequently referred to it, their policy of "non-alliance." The Norwegians and the Danes were pursuing essentially the same policy, and in both countries it was referred to as "bridgebuilding."[22] The three countries, however, were pursuing the same policy in practice even if the intellectual foundations were different, for if the Swedes were opposed to blocbuilding *because* of their neutrality or non-alliance policy, the Norwegians and the Danes were likewise opposed to politico-military blocs *in order to* strengthen the foundations of the United Nations. Nevertheless the co-operation that did exist was not institutionalized nor did it involve any future commitments on the part of any. It was rather a co-operation based on political expediency and on the sense of community that existed among the Scandinavian states and, later, their common Social Democratic (Labor) governments.[23]

A turning point in the early postwar period came in June, 1947, with General Marshall's speech at Harvard offering American assistance to the European reconstruction effort. Norway, along with the other Scandinavian countries, accepted the invitation to attend the meeting of the Committee on European Economic Assistance in Paris in July of 1947, although their participation was cautious, as is indicated by the fact that they sent ambassadorial level representatives to the first preparatory meetings (unlike the other participating countries, which sent their foreign ministers). Although the three later became members of the Organization for European Economic Cooperation and were recipients of Marshall aid,[24] it is clear that they were concerned, at least in the beginning, that through economic co-operation they might compromise the prerequisites of their respective foreign policies.[25]

Other events of significance were also occurring in the international milieu. Churchill, early in 1946, delivered his famous "Iron Curtain" speech at Fulton, Missouri.[26] One year later the U.S. President announced the Truman Doctrine,[27] and throughout this period it was obvious to most observers that serious differences existed among the great powers as witnessed by their failure to achieve results at the peace conferences, the denunciation of the Marshall Plan by the Soviet Union accompanied by the refusal of the Soviet bloc countries to participate, and the establishment of the Cominform.[28]

These and many other "objective" environmental events would seem to indicate that all was not well among the great powers. Both the British and the Americans and the U.S.S.R. had by late 1947 recognized the formation of politico-security blocs, and even the Swedes had made similar public observations. The new Norwegian Foreign Minister, however, refused to recognize the "reality" that was affirmed by most journalists and politicians around the world, and he continued to perceive international political conditions in a manner that would permit the United Nations to function as a security organization.

On January 20, 1948, in a general debate occasioned by the Foreign Minister's report to the Storting in December, 1947, Foreign Minister Lange restated clearly the Norwegian perception of international events, an evaluation that had prevailed since the end of the war. Although some members of the Storting were concerned about the state of affairs in international politics, Lange said that, viewed in a historical perspective, the tension that was felt by all and reported daily in the newspapers was "more a post-war tension than a prelude to a new order." [29] Thus there was no need for change in the main lines of Norwegian foreign policy and the greatest contribution that Norway could make toward a stable international situation would be continued progress with the program for reconstruction, or, as he said, "putting our own house in order."

Although the Foreign Minister recognized that the times were difficult, he said that there was no question of Norway's choosing sides because such a question "assumes that one believes that a warlike settlement is not to be avoided, and that cannot and must not be the basis for Norwegian foreign policy.[30]

Two weeks following Lange's statements to the Storting, the Defense Minister,[31] in a policy statement to the Storting on the state of Norway's defenses and related budget problems, quoted Lange's admonition that the Norwegian contribution to international stability would best be served by putting its own house in order[32] and in general reaffirmed the broad evaluation of the international situation as made by the Foreign Minister, viz., that Norway was not threatened and that the bases and assumptions of Norwegian defense planning remained valid.[33]

These two speeches are all the more significant when it is

recalled that two days after Lange's evaluation and prior to the Defense Minister's, Foreign Minister Bevin made his now famous speech in the House of Commons evaluating the contemporary international situation and proposing the unification of Western Europe. He said that the trend of events in Europe was now clear beyond doubt and that the Western nations were faced with a *fait accompli* in Eastern Europe and therefore "the free nations of Western Europe must draw closely together (and) we are thinking now of Western Europe as a unit." [34]

The asymmetry between the Norwegian and British perception of the present and predictions about the future are here seen in bold relief, but, in view of what has been said above about Norway's foreign policy, it is obvious that an interpretation by the Norwegian government of the many environmental events as anything other than "temporary tensions" would have undermined the entire basis of its foreign and security policy and would have required a complete re-examination and modification of the three-year defense plan. [35]

It should be noted here that the Bevin speech made quite an impact in Scandinavia, and especially in Sweden. Many at first linked the Bevin proposals to the Marshall Plan. This interpretation was made by some in Scandinavia and by the Russians. The Russians held that the Bevin speech was an affront to the Soviet Union, and they stated in *Pravda* on January 25, 1948, that the Americans were behind the ideas presented by Bevin since American strategic plans, as proposed by Defense Minister Forrestal, envisioned a well-organized Western Europe to provide military bases for the U.S. [36] The Russians further charged that the Bevin Plan intended to draw in the Scandinavian countries through the instrument of the Marshall Plan. [37] Although Bevin did not name any of the Scandinavian countries in his talk, it was suggested in Norway, and it had been reported unofficially in London, that the Nordic countries could have a place in the inchoate arrangements if they wanted it. [38] Some of the bourgeoise papers in Norway began to suggest that the Scandinavian countries were now required to take a hard look at their foreign policies and perhaps revise them; some, in fact, indicated that the time had come to choose sides. [39]

Although the first official reaction from Scandinavia came from Denmark,[40] the most important reaction was that of the Swedish Foreign Minister because of the response it elicited from Foreign Minister Lange. Swedish Foreign Minister Undén stated in a foreign affairs debate in the Riksdag on February 4, 1948, that Sweden did not wish to join *any* bloc.[41] If the United Nations fails, Undén said that Sweden must have the option of choosing the way of neutrality.[42]

Undén later denied that his speech was in any way directed toward Bevin's proposals; nevertheless his remarks were widely interpreted as Sweden's (and probably Scandinavia's) answer to Bevin. It is within this context that Lange's speech to the Storting on February 12, 1948, is significant. There the Foreign Minister affirmed that Norway had not been invited to take part in the European arrangement envisioned by Bevin, but he also went to great lengths to convince the Storting (and probably his other publics, both domestic and foreign) that Undén had not necessarily spoken for Norway. Lange said, with reference to Undén's speech in the Riksdag and to the interpretation that it had been given in the American and British press, that "Nordic cooperation . . . is not of the variety that one speaks for all." [43] He said that on many questions the Scandinavian countries were able to take the same position, and he admitted that there was much in their histories that was common. But he warned that at the present time important "nuances" existed in their respective policies and that the countries' historical experiences had been different, "not the least in the latest years." In the same speech the Foreign Minister duly chastised the press for irresponsibly creating apprehension and fear that tended to create tensions, making more difficult wise judgments concerning the "genuine" risks in the present situation.

Thus, while Lange did not by any means endorse the Bevin Plan, he clearly indicated that he did not want to foreclose in advance any particular future course of action, and he stated without equivocation that Sweden did not speak for Norway.

Lange concluded his views with a statement about the United Nations. He recognized that the UN, as a result of the tensions that existed among the great powers, had "little ability to solve its central political problems." He added however that Norway must work from the assumption that the UN would succeed in overcoming its contradictions, making co-operation possible.[44] In the meantime Norway must seriously consider and re-examine its position, but such deliberations take time and require responsibility. Lange thus affirmed that Norwegian foreign policy, based on the UN, had not changed, although he gave no indication that it would not and agreed with those who suggested that it required serious reconsideration. So, even though Norwegian policy was clearly based on calculated judgments (however dogmatically adhered to) about the nature of the political circumstances in which Norway found herself, the Foreign Minister, while placating his critics, was not going to be forced into abandoning his chosen policy by admitting the political demise of the UN or by recognizing a grave threat to Norwegian security that would seem to call for arrangements more concrete and dependable than those provided by the United Nations.

It is interesting to note here parenthetically that both of these judgments were central to Norwegian foreign policy. For (1) if the UN were perceived as irrevocably paralyzed or (2) if the policy elite perceived a direct threat to the country, a new security policy would be required since Norway's defenses, as the Defense Minister had earlier admitted openly, were inadequate.[45] In passing, it is also interesting to note that such judgments were not central to Swedish foreign policy planners since the Swedes' policy of armed neutrality did not require (although it did not preclude) a strong and effective United Nations playing a central role in Swedish security policy. The effectiveness of the UN was central to Norwegian security policy however, and now even the Foreign Minister had publicly recognized its weaknesses; nevertheless, he maintained that Norway would continue to work for great power co-operation, i.e., continue the bridge-building policy. On the other hand, with this public recognition of the situation in the UN, it is clear that a perception of a threat to Norway would completely undermine the basis of Norwegian policy.

It is against this background that certain events in the international milieu must be seen. On February 23, 1948, the Communist party in Czechoslovakia gained control of the government through a coup d'état. This event had a great impact in Norway for several reasons: (1) Czechoslovakia, like Norway and Denmark, was an exponent of the bridgebuilding policy, (2) Jan Masaryk had only recently visited Norway, where he made a profound impression and was admired and respected throughout the country, and (3) a deep-rooted cultural relationship existed between the two countries, dating back to the nineteenth century when the Norwegians struggling for independence identified closely with the Czechoslovakian independence movement.[46] In addition, late in February the Soviet Union initiated talks with Finland that led to the signing in early April of the Treaty of Friendship, Cooperation, and Mutual Assistance,[47] and in the middle of March [48] the pact creating the Western Union was initialed in Brussels, and on March 31 the Soviets imposed strict controls on the movement of traffic to and from Berlin after having withdrawn from all Allied administrative committees in the city. Finally, on the domestic front Norway found itself in the midst of a crisis, stimulated in part by the events in Finland and to some extent press-inspired, involving alleged rumors about Soviet intentions to request a non-aggression pact with Norway (the so-called Easter Crisis of 1948).[49] In the meantime the government and the Storting had reacted to events by providing in March an extraordinary defense appropriation [50] and by appointing in April a "Special Committee for Foreign Policy and Defense Preparedness" that excluded the Communist Parliamentarians and for all practical purposes assumed the consultative and decision-making functions of the regular Foreign Affairs Committee.[51]

It is in this politically charged atmosphere that the Foreign Minister addressed the Oslo Military Society on April 19, 1948, providing an extensive evaluation of the international situation. In his speech to the Military Society Lange engaged in a very subtle and complex argumentation, which involved Norway's view toward the United Nations, an evaluation of the events in Czechoslovakia and Finland, and an indication of future intentions.

Because of the acknowledged weakness of the UN in his

previous major address, most important in the immediate context was the view expressed of events in Czechoslovakia and Finland. With regard to the former, the Foreign Minister said that the coup had not altered the situation in Europe from the strategic point of view, but rather its significance lay in its political and psychological impact. He said that it showed that the Czech Communists, in accordance with the constituent meeting of the Cominform, "had abandoned the idea that it should be possible to build a bridge between East and West, between Communism and Democracy," [52] and that the European Communist parties supported the coup demonstrated that they were not committed to democracy.

Next, he turned to the events in Finland, imparting a defensive motive for Soviet action, saying that the note "showed that the Soviet government was re-examining the question of securing itself militarily on its northern flank." [53] Lange said that because of these developments Norway had felt certain pressures, and he recognized that "rumors about Norway" abounded. He said that he did not think that Norway would be requested to sign a military agreement with the U.S.S.R., notwithstanding the sharp attack on the country in *Izvestia* on Easter evening. [54] Nevertheless he felt constrained to add that he "was certain that the Norwegian people are in agreement with the government that Norway cannot enter into a special military agreement with the Soviet Union." Thus he made clear Norway's position vis-à-vis the Soviet Union, and it is in this total effort to explain the Norwegian attitude and perhaps to pre-empt the Soviets diplomatically that he said, "There can be no doubt that we are a part of Western Europe, economically, geographically, and culturally, and we shall continue to be a Western European democracy." [55] That Lange saw a potential threat to Norway is suggested by the above and unquestionably implied by the following.

In the course of examining the Soviet-Finnish discussions and the "new risks" for Norway, the Foreign Minister said that he did not think that a general war was probable in the near future. However, real dangers did now exist for Norway, for it was always possible that a war might break out because of mutual fear or because one of the great powers might incorrectly evaluate the limits of provocation.[56] And in this regard an especially large danger existed in the possibility that a great power might "occupy a strategically important area which is undefended." In view of this fact, he said, Norway had recently increased its defense appropriation.[57] Again revealing the nature of his strategic thinking, Lange refused to condemn the Western Union as aggressive. Rather, he said,

such a consolidation can become a step in the direction of stabilizing relationships, a contribution to the shaping of a new equilibrium and basis for an independent contribution which can be able to counteract the severe tensions between the two leading great powers.[58]

Regarding the main lines of Norwegian foreign policy, the Foreign Minister said that Norway must continue to work for peaceful relations among states "with different social systems and different ideological views." Lange said that the UN continued to be the basis of Norwegian foreign policy,

and the main line of our foreign policy must continue to be our contribution in the United Nations and through its organs for peace, security, and international cooperation. We must continue to hope and work for a UN which shall be able to become an effective security organization.

But that the United Nations was not at this time an effective security organization was also clear:

. . . we must not shut our eyes to the fact that the UN today does not provide the member states with complete security.

Thus the Norwegian Foreign Minister's position was clarified. What began as an examination of the international situation concluded with a weak affirmation of Norway's bridgebuilding policy. Norway would continue to work for a strong United Nations, but dangers were now perceived to exist for Norway in view of her inadequate military capability and her strategic location. Although Lange did not mention the Soviet Union directly in connection with the threat to Norway, there is little room to doubt that he was thinking of the Soviets when he spoke of the danger created by inadequately defended strategic areas. He rejected, directly and explicitly and indirectly by implication, Norway's involvement in a security agreement with the Soviet Union. Such a position was consistent with, and could be predicted from, the policy of bridgebuilding, but earlier in his speech Lange declared, referring to the Bevin Plan, that "we will not preclude for ourselves the possibility of discussing a closer relationship with the West, both culturally and politically." [59] Thus while Lange rejected any such relationship with the Soviets, he left open the development of Norway's relationship with the West. In this regard, the Foreign Minister seriously compromised, at least verbally, the policy of bridgebuilding. At this point the remarks of the Foreign Minister about Scandinavia should be noted, for in a subtle way he indicated that Norway might not, unlike in past periods of tension and crisis, confine itself to Scandinavia. He said it was imperative "to search for a policy on which the three Northern countries can stand together," adding that

It shall take very weighty reasons before we shall choose a policy which can separate us from Denmark and Sweden or from one of them.[60]

That separation was a possibility, however, was clear, for the Norwegian Foreign Minister warned that the "politico-military problems of each of the three Scandinavian countries were not identical, and this fact can cause certain difficulties in the effort to find a common solution."

Thus, it appears that "bridgebuilding" remained in name only. Norway was watching closely international events and configurations. She had unambiguously articulated her posture and attitude toward the Soviet Union, and although she would not foreclose a future relationship with the newly-formed Western Union, she first hoped to find a common Scandinavian solution to her problem.

Norway was now committed to a search for new alternatives

in her foreign policy. The United Nations had always been perceived as weak, but this perception would not affect policy unless Norway were subjected to threats or danger. Lange in this speech defined, for the first time, the danger: a weak country occupying a strategically important area and thereby inviting a pre-emptive move by one or another of the major powers.[61] The foreign policy elite had viewed Norway as a strategically located country since the early war years and had on many occasions since 1946 publicly observed Norway's inability to defend herself without outside aid. Rising tensions thus increased the emphasis placed on the strategic importance of Norway's geographic position, and although Norway did not want to exacerbate relations among the great powers, her priorities had changed, for now the Foreign Minister said,

We want . . . under all circumstances to defend ourselves against attack, and we have the problem in our foreign policy to provide for obtaining for ourselves the greatest possible security against the danger of aggression.[62]

The United Nations was supposed to provide this security, and the policy of bridgebuilding was aimed at making the United Nations function as it was intended. Bridgebuilding had failed, from the beginning, but in the absence of specific threat Norway could continue to base her security on the United Nations Organization and bend all efforts toward making great power co-operation a reality, refraining from any action that might exacerbate great power relations. Now, however, she could not afford such restraint. Norway would continue to work for a strong and effective United Nations and great power co-operation, but in her search for security she would not automatically and necessarily refrain from actions that might increase tensions or that might be viewed unfavorably by one of the great power blocs. Also, Lange now revealed that he did not view blocs as necessarily destabilizing, and his conception of "political and military vacuums" indicated a concern for pre-emption and a concomitant primitive deterrent concept in his strategic thinking. A weak UN could be tolerated in the absence of a threat to Norwegian security. In the Military Society speech the Foreign Minister defined the threat for the first time. The threat defined did not specify a particular country but rather was stated in terms of a *situation* arising out of Norway's particular geographic location coupled with prevailing international conditions. A weak UN and a threat situation together were intolerable.

1. See, for example, Halvdan Koht, *Norway Neutral and Invaded* (London: Hutchinson, 1941), chap. vii, pp. 189–96, where he discusses Norwegian war aims in terms of "peace with liberty and independence." His views do not go beyond this aim for the postwar world, except he does argue that the peace must be made secure against other aggressions from the Nazis, but this, he says, "is first and foremost a task for the German nation." Koht seemed to envision a "business as usual" arrangement after the war.

2. Finn Moe, *Norge i den nye Verden* (Oslo: Tiden, 1946), p. 43.

3. On this see Helge Giverholt, "North Norway in International Politics," *Norseman*, XII (January–February, 1954), 1–6, for a thorough discussion of the significance of North Norway and the Svalbard archipelago in international politics. For a controversial view of North Norway in world politics see Nils Ørvik, *Europe's Northern Cap and the Soviet Union* (Cambridge: Harvard Center for International Affairs, Occasional Papers No. 6, 1963), *passim.*

4. This alteration of priorities can probably be attributed to two factors: Russia's entry into the war and realization that Germany was not going to be in a position to pose a threat to Norway for many years to come. Thus the strategic emphases were modified. These points are made explicit by Wilhelm Keilhau, "Norway and the Atlantic Pact," *Norseman*, VII (March–April, 1949), 80; and Wilhelm Keilhau, "Britain and Norway: A Survey of Mutual Relations," *Norseman*, XI (January–February, 1953), 6–7.

5. For a good yet brief discussion of these problems see Per Kleppe, *Main Aspects of Economic Policy in Norway since the War* (Oslo: Oslo University Press, 1960), pp. 1–12; and Erik Brofoss, *Survey of Economic Developments and of Economic Policies in Norway since World War II* (Oslo: University of Oslo International Summer School, 1963), pp. 5–8.

6. The main objectives: full employment, rising living standards, fair distribution of income, and reconstruction and development of the means of production, were outlined to the Storting in general terms in November, 1945, and specifically in the form of a government White Paper in February, 1946.

7. Among those who have so described postwar Norwegian foreign policy are Brita Skottsberg Åhman, "Scandinavian Foreign Policy, Past and Present," in Henning Friis, *Scandinavia between East and West* (Ithaca: Cornell University Press, 1950), p. 295; Wilfred Ryder, "The End of Nordic Neutrality," *Soundings*, XXIV (March, 1949), 15; John Midgaard, *A Brief History of Norway* (Oslo: Nikolai Olsens Boktrykkeri, 1963), p. 140; Leroy Karlstrøm, "Beginning and End of Norwegian Neutrality," *Norseman*, IX

(September–October, 1951), 293; Nils Ørvik, *The Decline of Neutrality* (Oslo: Johan Grundt Forlag, 1953), pp. 257–58, although Ørvik takes a different position in his later monograph entitled *Trends in Norwegian Foreign Policy* (Oslo: Norwegian Institute of International Affairs, 1962), p. 20. For a hedging characterization see Keilhau, *op. cit.*, pp. 80–81. For a good example of the view suggested here, see John Sanness, "Norway, An Outsider at Paris," *Norseman,* IV (November–December, 1946), 431–35; and paradoxically since he is concerned primarily with domestic politics, James A. Storing, *Norwegian Democracy* (Oslo: Universitetsforlaget, 1963), chap. xii, esp., p. 213.

8. See *Infra,* Appendix A; the Nygaardsvold government resigned on June 12, 1945, having governed Norway since March 20, 1935. Chief Justice and Home Front leader Paul Berg was requested to form a provisional government following the voluntary dissolution of the government; however, he was unable to do so to the satisfaction of the major political parties. Finally, on June 22, Einar Gerhardsen, Laborite Mayor of Oslo, succeeded in forming a new coalition government which served until the Parliamentary elections on October 8, 1945, which gave Labor an undisputable mandate. Gerhardsen remained the leader of the government after the elections.

9. The Labor party formed a minority government in 1936 with parliamentary support of the Agrarian party. This government remained in power until the war. During the war and immediately after it the Labor party was in charge of coalition governments in which all major parties participated.

10. Ryder, *op. cit.,* pp. 16–17.

11. Sanness, *op. cit.,* p. 432; Alexander Werth, "This is Scandinavia," *Nation,* CLXXIII (October, 1951), 295, cites the sympathy for the U.S.S.R. which prevailed in the left wing of the Labor party.

12. On this point see the remarks in *Instilling fra Forsvarskommisjonen av 1946,* Part I (Oslo: Arbeidernes Aktietrykkeri, 1949), pp. 13–14.

13. Lie's speech quoted in Einar Løchen and Rolf N. Torgersen, *Norway's Views on Sovereignty* (Bergen: Chr. Michelsens Institutt, 1955), pp. 39 ff.

14. Lie took the oath as Secretary-General of the United Nations on February 2, 1946.

15. Lange, named Foreign Minister on February 1, 1946, was an acknowledged leader in the Labor party and one of the top men in the home front leadership, although he spent much time in concentration camps in Germany. Prior to the war, he had advocated greater attention to arms for defense and more support of the League's collective security system. Lange had a great deal of exposure to international life traveling with his father, Nobel Prize winner Chr. Lange, living much of his life abroad in London, Germany, and The Hague. See *Norway Digest,* No. 6, (February 8, 1946); *News of Norway,* VI, No. 18 (February, 1949), 71.

16. See Lange's radio speech to the Norwegian people on February 4, 1946, in Halvard Lange, *Norsk Utenrikspolitikk siden 1945* (Oslo: Johan Grundt Tanum, 1952), p. 13.

17. Tormod P. Svennivig, "The Scandinavian Bloc at the UN and Its New Outlook," *Norseman,* XIII (May–June, 1955), 146; see also Thomas Hovet, *Bloc Politics in the United Nations* (Cambridge: Harvard University Press, 1960), pp. 73–76; for an indication of the cohesiveness of the Scandi-

navian bloc at the UN see Charts 31–36 in Hovet. During the first three meetings of the General Assembly (four sessions), the Scandinavian bloc was divided on fewer than 8 per cent of the votes.

18. A good example of the proposals for a Scandinavian defense arrangement from the Norwegian side can be seen in Johan Vogt, *Russland og Norden* (Oslo: Aschehoug, 1945). Vogt's proposals were based primarily on strategic considerations which enjoyed wide currency in Scandinavia, viz., Soviet foreign policy was primarily aimed at securing her frontiers, and that Russian policy toward the North has always attempted to insure that the area would not become a springboard for attack. Thus both for their own security and in the interests of world peace the Scandinavian countries would be well advised to establish their own defense system without any anti-Russian elements and preclude a great power foothold on the backdoor of the U.S.S.R.

19. This skepticism toward blocs in general and the reluctance to join any bloc undoubtedly encouraged many observers to characterize postwar Norwegian foreign policy as a "return to neutrality."

20. See *Norway Digest,* January 18, 1946, and August 3, 1945.

21. Denmark was, in this and other matters, usually the strongest proponent of a "Scandinavian arrangement" and probably for much the same reason as in the middle of the nineteenth century. For an academician's view of these problems which corresponded closely to the official Norwegian view see Arnold Wolfers, "In Defense of Small Countries," *Yale Review,* XXXIII (Winter, 1943), 201–20.

22. For a brief discussion of Danish foreign policy during this period see Sven Henningsen, "The Foreign Policy of Denmark," in Joseph E. Black and Kenneth W. Thompson (eds.), *Foreign Policies in a World of Change* (New York: Harper & Row, 1963), pp. 100, 102; and Erik Reske-Nielsen and Erik Kragh, *Atlantpagten og Danmark* (København: Atlantsammenslutningen, 1962), p. 30.

23. The Social Democrats assumed power in Denmark in the 1947 elections. The significance of personal relationships and common Labor governments in postwar Scandinavian foreign policy discussions is cited in Keilhau, "Norway and the Atlantic Pact," p. 83.

24. Norway, which had rather large reserves of foreign currencies at the end of the war and a large foreign loan capability, had originally planned to carry out reconstruction and stabilization programs without external assistance. This proved to have been a misjudgment and Norway received more than $460 million in direct and indirect assistance between April, 1948, and June, 1953. See Brofoss, *op. cit.,* pp. 27–29.

25. See Ryder, *op. cit.,* p. 16. This view persisted among the left wing of the Labor party, which opposed a close relationship with the U.S. for ideological, political and strategic reasons.

26. March 5, 1946.

27. March 12, 1947.

28. October 6, 1947.

29. *Stortingstidende,* "Debatten om utenriksministerens redegjørelse 11.12.47," January 20, 1948, pp. 43 ff.

30. *Ibid.,* p. 57.

31. Reference here is to Jens Chr. Hauge.

32. *Stortingstidende,* "Redegjørelse om forsvarets stilling," February 4, 1948, p. 119. The entire statement provides a good account of the aims of the three-year defense plan (1946–49).

33. *Ibid.,* p. 124.

34. See Halford Hoskins, *The Atlantic Pact* (Washington, D.C.: Public Affairs Press, 1949), p. 22. The response to Bevin's speech was immediate, and by February 19, 1948, the Draft Treaty for the Western Union was completed, and on March 17, 1948, it was initialed by Britain, France, and the Benelux countries.

35. See "Redegjørelse om forsvarets stilling," *op. cit.,* p. 124, for a statement of Hauge's low regard for the strength of Norwegian defenses.

36. "Reaksjonen på Bevin-planen," *Kontakt,* II (March, 1948), 11.

37. "Moskva fornøyd med Undéns tale," *Kontakt,* II (March, 1948), 11.

38. "Bevin-planen og de nordiske land," *Kontakt,* II (March, 1948), 11–12.

39. *Ibid.,* p. 11.

40. Prime Minister Hans Hedtoft said in a radio interview in January, 1948, that "Denmark will attach itself neither to an East bloc nor a West bloc. It cannot be in Scandinavia's interest to patronize the unfortunate contradictions which today prevail between the great power groups."

41. Undén said, "We must be free to choose the path of neutrality if the new security organization is unable to act. We do not wish, by an agreement reached in advance, to surrender the right to stand aloof from a new war."

42. In London and in other capitals, Undén's speech was widely interpreted as a rejection of the Bevin plan. And those in London felt constrained to point out that Bevin was not including Sweden or Denmark in his proposals in the first place. Undén had created a small crisis and replied that London had misunderstood his remarks, that he was not referring to the Bevin plan at all, but was rather addressing himself to a domestic audience. On this see also "Bevin-planen og de nordiske land," p. 12.

43. Lange, *op. cit.,* pp. 55. The occasion was the debate on the annual Speech from the Throne.

44. *Ibid.,* p. 59.

45. Hauge said in the Storting, "The defense capability which the country will have built up at the end of the three-year plan cannot be characterized as strong either in the military or civil sectors. . . ." See also Tim Greve, *Norway and NATO* (Oslo: Oslo University Press, 1959), p. 7.

46. On these points see Karlstrøm, *op. cit.,* p. 294; and Tim Greve and Jakob Sverdrup, *NATO gjennon ti År* (Oslo: Aschehoug, 1959), p. 103.

47. Although this Treaty ties Finland closely to the Soviet Union, it differs considerably (in Finland's favor) from similar treaties signed by the Soviets with their other Eastern European neighbors. Nevertheless, the Treaty commits Finland to avoid involvement in great power conflicts and to ward off attacks by Germany or her allies either unilaterally or in concert with the U.S.S.R. Until 1955 and the "thaw" in the Soviet Union, Finland remained an outsider in international affairs. See Erik Castren, "Peace Treaties and

98 • *Elite Images and Foreign Policy Outcomes*

Other Agreements Made by Finland," in Risto Hyvärinen, *et al.*, *Finnish Foreign Policy* (Helsinki: Finnish Foreign Policy Association, 1963), p. 62; Ralf Törngren, "The Neutrality of Finland," *Foreign Affairs*, XXXIX (July, 1961), 601–9, for an excellent discussion of Finland's foreign policy and related problems; and H. P. Krosby, "The Communist Power Bid in Finland," *Political Science Quarterly*, 75:229–43, 1960.

48. The Treaty linking France, the U.K., and Benelux was signed on March 17, 1948.

49. It was at first suspected in Scandinavia that the crisis was engineered by the U.S. Department of State in order to persuade the Scandinavians to join the Western bloc. These suspicions are plausible in view of statements made in the U.S. by the President and other members of the administration. See the *New York Times*, March 17, 1948, where it is hinted that U.S. aid might not extend to countries beyond the Western Union and the *New York Times*, March 18, 1948, where Truman referred to Finland and the "hazard" of Scandinavia. On the other hand, one observer has suggested that the Easter Crisis may have resulted from an error in the Norwegian Foreign Office: "On learning of Stalin's letter to President Paasikivi of Finland, Foreign Minister Halvard Lange of Norway cabled his Moscow Ambassador to ask if the Russians intended to approach Norway next. The Ambassador replied briefly that the Soviet Union had always wanted a non-aggression pact with Norway—which was quite true. The reply was garbled in transmission and wrongly deciphered to read that one was wanted now. Lange at once told the British and American Ambassadors in Oslo, who, on the instructions of their governments did in fact advise the three states to be ready for an approach by the Soviet Union, with all that it implied if refused." On this see Ryder, *op. cit.*, p. 17; see also Keith Hutchison, "Scandinavia between the Blocs," *Nation*, CLXVII (July, 1948), 67–69; and Greve, *op. cit.*, p. 8.

50. The appropriation of 100 m. kroner ($20 million in 1948 kroner) was granted on March 12, 1948.

51. Although the President of the Storting gave as the official reason the desire to have defense and foreign policy matters examined by the same group, it was a thinly veiled attempt to remove Communists from the discussion of foreign and defense policy matters in order to maintain confidence between the government and the foreign policy elite in the Storting. The eleven Communists in the Storting severely criticized the new Committee, but it was not abolished until January, 1950—after the decision to join NATO had been made and after the total defeat of the Communists in the 1949 parliamentary election. See *Infra*, Appendix A; see also Einar Løchen, *Norway in European and Atlantic Cooperation* (Oslo: Universitetsforlaget, 1964), pp. 73–74.

52. Lange, *op. cit.*, p. 62.

53. *Ibid.*

54. *Ibid.*, p. 64.

55. *Ibid.*, p. 61. This phrase is almost always cited by Norwegian foreign policy analysts as indicative of her future course of action vis-à-vis the West. As will be more fully developed later, it seems clear that the statement was probably (and certainly logically) aimed more toward the Soviet Union and was relative to the "rumors" about a Soviet desire for a special agreement with Norway than it was revealing of future Norwegian foreign policy moves.

56. *Ibid.*, p. 63.

57. See *supra*, n. 50, this chapter.

58. Lange, *op. cit.*, pp. 66 ff.

59. *Ibid.*, p. 61. Lange made it very clear, however, that no plans were being made to include Norway in the Western Union.

60. *Ibid.*, p. 64.

61. It is interesting to note that Lange's argumentation did not involve (nor did it logically require) a view of Soviet foreign policy as aggressive (a view, which if it existed, would have represented a revision of the image of the U.S.S.R.). As has been pointed out above, the Norwegians persisted in their view of postwar Soviet actions as having a defensive-security, not expansionist, motivation. Lange said nothing to indicate that this view had been altered. Nevertheless, a danger existed for Norway because the tensions and fears which prevailed in international politics might induce a great power to occupy a strategically important, yet undefended territory. That such circumstances might develop was not unprecedented and was supported by Norway's historical experience since this is essentially what had occurred in 1940, with pre-emptive arguments salient in the documents both from the German and British sides. Some critics of Lange felt that Norwegian leaders were obsessed with the experience of the German invasion and referred to this concern as the "Ninth of April complex in Norwegian politics." This charge was made by the editor of *Kontakt* in Torolf Elster, "Norges utenrikspolitiske stilling," *Økonomi og Politik* (Copenhagen), XXV (1951), 125.

62. Lange, *op. cit.*, p. 64.

UNIVERSITY OF VICTORIA
LIBRARY
Victoria, B. C.

~~~~~~~

CHAPTER IV

The Search for Security:
Scandinavia and the Atlantic

The security problem in perspective.—As the preceding discussion has suggested, by the spring of 1948 Norwegian leaders perceived their nation as threatened and perceived the United Nations as unable to provide the member states with a satisfactory measure of security. Two points should be recalled. One, Norway had from the beginning looked to the UN as the basis of her security policy: the so-called policy of bridgebuilding was nothing more than an attempt to make the UN function as a security organization.[1] That the Norwegians became almost totally absorbed with their domestic problems, added to the imperatives of the bridgebuilding policy, tended to obscure the fundamental fact that they were determined to insure against "another 1940." In fact, the Norwegians prosecuted an active security policy that looked to the UN as the primary instrument. Second, the threat that was perceived by the Norwegian policy elite was expressed in terms of a "threat situation" (i.e., the danger to Norway resulting from her strategic location, her inability to defend herself, and the tensions that prevailed in international politics) rather than in terms of a "threat from" a specified country. In the development of the Norwegian strategic image during the spring of 1948 it is clear that the crucial variable was the presence or absence of a threat to Norwegian security;[2] once such a threat was perceived, as it was by the Foreign Minister in his April address, the corner was turned. Now, if Norway were primarily concerned with national security, that is, if physical security over the short run were her highest priority, a new security policy orientation would have to be found, and for the next twelve months the Norwegian government would be concerned with finding an acceptable solution to its security dilemma.

In this search the Norwegians had *in theory* at least six clear alternatives: (1) a return to an independent neutrality as in the years 1936–40; (2) a policy of collective security, based on the ability of the UN to function as a security organization; (3) an alliance or similar agreement with the Soviet Union; (4) an alliance with the Western bloc;[3] (5) an alliance with the Scandinavian bloc; and (6) membership in a Scandinavian bloc as a subsystem within a larger Western bloc. However, examined within the framework of the development of the Norwegian strategic image as well as in recognition of related policy statements, it is clear that these options, which existed in theory, did not exist within the range of relevant alternatives.

The first option, a return to an independent neutrality policy, was obviously impossible without a radical revision of her strategic image,[4] and there is no evidence that this revision had occurred or was in the process of taking place. The second option, a continuation of her postwar foreign policy, had just been discredited by the Foreign Minister as insufficient. The third option likewise had been rejected explicitly, when the Foreign Minister stated that Norway would not enter into a special military agreement with the Soviets. On the other hand, the fourth option was open; Lange had observed that Norway would not exclude the possibility of a closer political relationship with the West. The remaining two options were problematical; very little had been said in public by anyone regarding the establishment of a Scandinavian bloc within a larger Western arrangement. And although much had been said in very general terms about the possibilities of an independent Scandinavian arrangement, an analysis of the Norwegian strategic image would seem to indicate that such an arrangement was unlikely.

Thus it must be concluded that the articulated image of the international political universe and Norway's place in it had reduced the six theoretical options to two: Norwegian membership in a Scandinavian bloc attached to a Western arrangement or direct Norwegian membership in the Western bloc.

Prelude to the Scandinavian defense negotiations.—Notwithstanding the fact that the Norwegian strategic image did not seem to encourage the option of an isolated Scandinavian defense bloc, much discussion prevailed in all three countries concerning the possibilities of such an arrangement. Indeed, Lange had seemed to encourage such speculation in April when he said that it would take "weighty reasons" to make Norway choose a policy line different from Denmark or Sweden.[5]

In any case, it is now known that much was going on behind the scenes with regard to the possibility of a future defense arrangement among the three Scandinavian countries. Late in April, the Swedish government presented its proposals regarding the formation of a three nation defense pact to the Swedish Advisory Council on Foreign Affairs, which subsequently approved the plans.[6] And in early May, when the Swedish Foreign Minister was in Oslo, the question of a Scandinavian defense alliance was discussed with Norwegian officials,[7] although the first public suggestion that such discussions were in progress did not come until May 9, 1948.[8]

It is against this background of events that Lange delivered his next major foreign policy address in June in Malmö, Sweden. Although the greater part of the address was focused on problems connected with Scandinavian economic co-operation, the Foreign Minister offered significant comment on Scandinavian foreign and security policy problems. In the course of discussing the difficult problems encountered in closer Scandinavian co-operation the Foreign Minister observed that intra-Scandinavian differences were most sharply revealed when Scandinavians turned to questions of foreign policy and evaluations of security and defense problems.[9] He pointed out that these differences of view, especially the value to be placed on defense, had long existed and were responsible for the fact that military co-operation had never been "seriously considered." Lange observed that the experience of the war was important, especially for Denmark and Norway, in leading them to view differently the sacrifices that were required for national defense. Lange then said that great advantages could be gained for the Scandinavian countries if they could achieve some form of peacetime "practical coordination in the defense of our three countries." [10] However, the Foreign Minister added parenthetically that

I am not thinking in terms of a direct politico-military agreement, but of practical coordination. [11]

The Foreign Minister added, moreover, that it is best to admit "that today a common Scandinavian policy cannot be found for the main questions of foreign policy, at least in the short run." This summing up of the political situation in Scandinavia followed a very revealing evaluation which indicates that some discussion among the three countries concerning defense cooperation and foreign policy had taken place, for the Foreign Minister had said,

But nothing is gained by overlooking that the different experiences of our three countries during the war have created a different atmosphere regarding the attitude toward the main contemporary foreign policy questions in Norway, Sweden, and Denmark.

Apart from the impact of historical experience which was perceived as having an effect on the different views of the three countries, the Foreign Minister stated another reason for the differences which prevailed (a reason and construction that was to be heard more often in the months to come).

In addition there is a genuine difference in the strategic situation of our three countries. Both of these factors [i.e., historical experience and the strategic "situation"] lead to dissimilarities in the evaluation of the risk factors we face in the present and the near future international situation, and a different appraisal of which way we ought to follow in order to meet the dangers we face, of which way we ought to go for the best possible and most effective contribution for preventing war in the future. There are also differences in the appraisals among our countries concerning the possibilities we have to keep out of war, if the catastrophe we all see as the main task of preventing should nevertheless come.[12]

Thus Lange stated the Norwegian appraisal of the issues. Two factors were judged to be fundamental: historical experience and strategic location. From these two were derived judgments about the present and predictions about the future, judgments that apparently were not shared in the other Scandinavian foreign ministries.

The position of Sweden and Denmark.—Although the central concern here is with the development of Norwegian policy and the evolution of the Norwegian strategic image, it is useful to examine briefly the views of Denmark and Sweden toward the evolving international situation in general and the possibility of a Scandinavian security alignment specifically.

The position of Denmark can be dealt with most easily. Denmark, like Norway, had pursued a bridgebuilding policy since the war, and, again like Norway, had experienced disaster with her policy of neutrality in April of 1940.[13] The Danes, however, did not react to the events of early 1948 in the same manner as the Norwegians, nor were they so quick to underwrite Western "bloc-building." The Danes have always been the strongest proponents of pan-Scandinavianism, and when it became clearer that the UN could not be depended on as a security organization, and, perhaps more importantly, when the Norwegians began to equivocate their bridgebuilding policy, Denmark began a "Scandinavia lobby." If any blocs were going to be formed outside the United Nations, Denmark wanted a Scandinavian bloc. This aim was unconditional and expressed by the Foreign Minister in early June, 1948.

The Government regards it as its foremost task to try to further Northern understanding and ensure that the ways of the Scandinavian countries shall not separate.[14]

Although the Danes had little to offer a Scandinavian defense arrangement, the Danish Prime Minister [15] became its most outspoken advocate. As events unfolded, however, the differences of opinion in the North were between Norway and Sweden; thus, in short, it can be said without too much distortion that the Danish role was that of mediator between Norway and Sweden and that Danish views were not really germane to the decisive issues in the debate about "Scandinavia."

It is interesting to note in passing that Denmark's position vis-à-vis Germany and her control of the Baltic exits place her in a position that would seem to preclude, from the point of view of military-strategic considerations, her inclusion in any attempt to solve the security problems of Norway and Sweden. This is a fact of life with which the Danes have always lived and is expressed by the old saw in Danish foreign policy thinking that "politically Denmark belongs to Scandinavia but strategically to the Continent." The ability of a Norwegian-Swedish alliance to "keep outside" a war might be argued, but with Denmark attached, the probability of non-involvement seems to be much more remote.[16] Important as this consideration is, however, no evidence exists to the effect that a bilateral Norwegian-Swedish arrangement without Denmark was ever officially contemplated.[17]

As suggested above, the decisive issues in the Scandinavian debate of foreign and defense policies were between Norway and Sweden. As the Norwegian Foreign Minister had implied in his addresses, Sweden's experiences in international affairs had been much different from those of Norway. Sweden, since the first Bernadotte, had pursued successfully, although not without great difficulty,[18] a policy of neutrality. Sweden's neutrality policy later was referred to as a policy of non-alliance in peace that looked to non-involvement in war.[19] Regardless of how it is characterized, however, the "lesson" of history can be seen in that this policy kept the Swedes out of war for more than one hundred and thirty-five years, and it succeeded in World War II when Denmark's and Norway's failed.

As previously stated, during World War II the Swedes engaged in some discussion of the desirability of close Scandinavian co-operation, including political and defense co-operation, following the war.[20] These proposals, however, were spurned by Norway, and after the war they were given no official expression as Sweden joined the United Nations, continuing her policy of armed neutrality. The great debate that took place when Sweden joined the League was not repeated when she joined the UN. The Swedes favored the veto system in the Security Council because they saw it as a means of reconciling their non-alliance-neutrality policy with UN membership, guaranteeing that they would not become involved in a dispute where the great powers disagreed. In this regard it is interesting to note that the Swedes maintained that any change in the veto arrangement or any change in the permanent membership on the Security Council (e.g., the withdrawal of one of the great powers) would require Sweden to re-examine the entire basis of her UN policy. The point is that the policy of neutrality continued to serve as the touchstone of Swedish action in international affairs, and it was a policy that was, at all costs, to be maintained. Thus, very much unlike Norway, the UN was not central to Swedish foreign policy, and, again, unlike Norway, it was the maintenance of a specific policy rather than the calculation of the effects of alternative policies that formed the basis of Sweden's behavior in the postwar world.[21] These different bases of action were operationally insignificant as long as the Norwegians maintained their policy of bridgebuilding: both wanted to avoid entanglement in politico-military blocs. However, once the Norwegians began to search for a new security policy, the Swedes initiated discussions and finally offered a defense pact to Norway and Denmark in order to keep them out of a Western arrangement.[22]

The Swedish position with regard to non-alliance was somewhat modified by this step, although the Foreign Minister maintained that it was not inconsistent since "non-alliance" meant essentially "non-alliance with great powers." Thus is gained an insight into the political character of the northern bloc envisioned by the Swedes. There is no evidence to suggest that the Swedes were ever willing to compromise their attitude regarding the political orientation of a northern bloc, and the Foreign Minister left no room for doubt when he addressed the members of his own party in May. He said that the question of a northern arrangement required a great deal of consideration before any concrete decisions could be made, but he stated without equivocation that Sweden would not permit herself to be drawn into *indirect* relations with a great power grouping in a way that would require her to choose one side or the other in the event of a future war. The Foreign Minister stated,

Among those today who are interested in a Scandinavian agreement on cooperation are some who think that cooperation shall really mean the inclusion of the Scandinavians as a regional group in a West bloc; but it is clear that the Swedish government, which does not wish to join a West bloc is no less unwilling to do so via a Scandinavian Alliance.[23]

The kind of Scandinavian arrangement envisioned by the Swedes, as far as its political orientation was concerned, was clearly, as the Foreign Minister stated, "an independent group with a program to hold our countries outside of other power groupings." *In short, the Swedish policy of neutrality was to be extended to Norway and Denmark.*

Although no attempt has been made here to examine systematically the Swedish strategic image, it is unquestionably clear that the Swedes thought it possible to remain in peace in the midst of war; this was, after all, the "meaning" of their historical experience.[24] However, it was also a judgment based on their tradition and practice of armed neutrality, a self-confidence and sense of national efficacy expressed by the Defense Minister when he said that Swedish defense "justified the assumption . . . that small states do not lack the prospects to keep outside of war." [25] It is more difficult to generalize regarding her perception of her geographic location, a crucial component of the Norwegian image structure. However it does seem that the Swedes perceived themselves as occupying a strategically important part of the globe, but, as compared with the Norwegians, they drew different conclusions. Those responsible for foreign policy reasoned that if Scandinavia were of strategic importance, it would be so for both sides. Thus a foothold by one great power grouping would have destabilizing political consequences and was therefore to be avoided.[26]

Returning to the Norwegian Foreign Minister's Malmö address, it will be recalled that he emphasized two factors that separated the Scandinavian countries: historical experience and strategic location. From these two perceptions derived judgments about the present and predictions about the future. It is clear that the Norwegians felt that they were exposed to serious danger, a view apparently not shared by Sweden. With reference to the future, two considerations seemed uppermost in the mind of the Norwegian Foreign Minister: (1) the optimal strategy to guarantee national security relative to the risks inherent in the Norwegian view of the situation and (2) the optimal strategy to prevent a general war from breaking out. It is obvious that the policies required by each of these two strategies might be mutually exclusive, that is, the policy designed to provide maximum guarantees to national security in the event of war could very well involve courses of action that might exacerbate rather than mitigate the tensions in international politics. Lange's reference to the differences in historical experience suggests that Norway's primary consideration was with national security, and the Foreign Minister's reference to the different appraisals in Scandinavia regarding the best way both to meet the present dangers and to prevent war indicates that these two strategies were judged as mutually exclusive by the Swedes. However, it is clear that the Norwegian Foreign Minister did *not* judge the requirements for national security and peace to be mutually exclusive. He indicated once again the low probability he attached to the ability of Norway to escape involvement in a general conflict (a view obviously not shared by the Swedes). Rather in Lange's view, if the probability of non-involvement in war were low, if Norway were threatened, and if politico-military blocs were not perceived as destabilizing, it was then possible for Norway to maximize her national security without jeopardizing international peace. Thus, if the Swedes were emphasizing the need to pursue political goals designed to mitigate political tensions, the Norwegians by the summer of 1948 seemed to be concerned with the military weakness and vulnerability of a strategic area as itself tension-producing.

Still, notwithstanding the fundamental differences that existed between the two countries, on both the intellectual and policy levels, the discussion of a Scandinavian defense arrangement continued until September when, in a communiqué closing a Scandinavian foreign ministers meeting, it was announced that a decision had been made to investigate jointly the possibility of Scandinavian defense co-operation.[27] This concrete step was taken although the Norwegian and Swedish policy elites differed regarding (1) the seriousness of the current international situation, (2) the probability that the Scandinavian countries, or any one of them, could remain aloof from a future war should it occur, (3) the optimal strategy to minimize the dangers to their respective countries, and (4) the optimal strategy to minimize the possibility of another war in the system.

The period of the Scandinavian defense investigation.—It should be noted that during the summer of 1948 the U.S. Senate passed the so-called Vandenburg Resolution which promised more than simply moral support from the United States with regard to the concerted efforts toward security arrangements that were emerging in the Western world,[28] and shortly after its passage exploratory negotiations opened in Washington concerning the establishment of an Atlantic defense system.[29] Undoubtedly this caused some anxiety on the Swedish side because it was not improbable that Norway might join with the Atlantic powers, an act which, in the Swedish view, would have unpredictable, adverse consequences for Sweden's neutrality.[30] Thus, it is in this context that during the summer of 1948 the officials in the three Scandinavian countries were attempting to determine the framework within which an investigation regarding the possibilities of Scandinavian defense and military co-operation could be conducted. And, as previously mentioned, a decision was made in September to proceed with an investigation.

The communiqué which reported the decision of the Scandinavian foreign ministers to establish a Scandinavian defense investigation was vague, especially with regard to the political assumptions that were to be made and the nature of the discussions to be undertaken.

In the exchange of views which has taken place among the governments, it has been determined that there prevails, among other reasons owing to the different attitudes toward defense policy in the three countries, a certain dissimilarity of the view toward security policy questions.[31]

This much was discernible from the public discussion that had taken place since the beginning of 1948 in Scandinavia; however, notwithstanding these differences of view the foreign ministers now determined that the time was ripe for serious discussions of defense co-operation, for they added,

The Foreign Ministers have found nevertheless that the prerequisites exist for initiating a common exploration of the question of military cooperation among the three countries.

The nature of these prerequisites that were now judged to exist was not revealed by the communiqué nor by the discussion that immediately followed. It is absolutely clear that the Norwegians had not endorsed at any time during the preceding eight months the idea of an isolated Scandinavian bloc based on the Swedish concept of neutrality, and on the day following the foreign ministers' meeting the Swedish Prime Minister removed any doubt that might have otherwise existed regarding the position of the Swedes, saying that the political parties of Sweden were united on foreign policy and uncompromising in their opposition to participation in any European organization that would involve a military alliance with the Western powers.[32] Thus it is clear that the Swedes had not altered their political conditions for a Scandinavian defense arrangement, i.e., the condition of no connections with other great power groupings.

Nevertheless, following the September meeting of the foreign ministers, the Scandinavian Defense Ministers met in Oslo in mid-October to inaugurate a joint examination of the possibilities and conditions for defense co-operation among their three countries. There they appointed a joint exploratory committee, the Scandinavian Defense Commission, to carry on the investigation.[33]

The next statement by the Norwegians that was revealing of their assumptions came several days later when the Prime Minister spoke of the dangers of political vacuums (indicating a close relationship between his assumptions and those of the Foreign Minister):

In my opinion there is one way which the peace of the world can be secured, namely, through a Western Europe which is economically —and I would like to add, militarily strong. . . . We must have a Western Europe which offers no nourishment for either social or political insecurity.[34]

The ghost of 1940 was also referred to by the Prime Minister when he said, "We in Norway must now make a clear choice, and we must choose freedom. To the extent of our ability, we shall not again witness the ravaging of our land by foreign troops." [35]

Not until the end of October was there another major evaluation of the international political situation by the Foreign Minister. The Foreign Minister addressed the Storting, offering a general review of world affairs since the war and providing additional insight into the work of the Scandinavian Defense Commission. Lange observed that the cold war was being intensified and that Western demobilization trends had been reversed.[36] The Foreign Minister then turned to a review of postwar developments, noting that the tensions among the great powers had increased and indicating specifically his view that the American attempts to aid the reconstruction of Europe had been strongly opposed by the Communists. Lange then voiced solid support for the Marshall Plan and the Western Union, noting that the latter was entirely defensive, "shaped by the fear of Soviet expansion," and that the former hardly represented any motives of political or economic hegemony.

The Foreign Minister then reinforced some of his previously

stated views regarding the postwar world. He said it was clear that "modern war would bring devastation and ruin even for the victorious powers." Lange said that none of the great powers wanted war, and especially not the U.S.S.R., which had suffered so much in the last war. The danger rather was that the prevailing tensions had a tendency to increase distrust and enmity and that the isolation of the Soviet Union might lead to a self-fulfilling prophecy.[37] On the other hand, Lange repeated in different words his concept of the danger of war, a concept that had been developed and refined since the end of 1947.

There is reason to hope that the fear of the disaster which will attend another war will be strong enough to secure peace, but there is always the risk of an unexpected and unpremeditated explosion.[38]

With regard to the United Nations the Foreign Minister said that Norway would continue to participate actively because the UN was able to solve many problems,[39] but at the same time one of the problems it could not solve was the security dilemma of the member states.[40] Therefore great interest was being manifested by many countries in a system of regional agreements. In this respect Lange referred to the relationship of the Eastern European states to the U.S.S.R. and with each other, the Western Union, the Inter-American Union, and the emerging North Atlantic arrangement. He then said, however, that "the cooperation among the Scandinavian states does not today have the same character as any of those regional groups." Then, revealing somewhat the character of the Scandinavian Defense Commission's investigations, he said,

We are now examining how and to what degree it may be extended in the economic field, and also the possibilities present for cooperation in the area of military defense.[41]

However, even if the Scandinavian defense investigation was to provide information to aid in the evaluation of the efficacy of a Scandinavian defense arrangement, Lange included the caveat that was contained in his spring evaluation, namely, that even though it was "natural" for the Norwegians to think of defense co-operation with the other Scandinavian states in order to solve their security dilemma, their respective strategic positions [42] were different and they had all had different experiences in the last war; thus the others did not share Norway's evaluation of the "foreign policy situation" and the implications of its security problems.[43]

Finally some of the "determinants" of foreign policy cited by Lange should be noted. First, with reference to Norwegian participation in the Marshall Plan and the Organization for European Economic Cooperation, the Foreign Minister said it was because Norway geographically, economically, and culturally belonged in Western Europe, reaffirming the observation made in his April address to the Military Society. Second, in an interesting formulation, Lange said that Norway had a great interest in preventing war, citing four basic reasons: Norway's fundamental democratic view, its entire tradition in international politics, its dependency on international commerce and shipping for the maintenance of high domestic living standards, and Norway's exposed geographic position.

Early in December Lange stated that "the evaluation of the international situation serves as the background for any foreign policy" [44] and that Norway's first interest was in peace, but that under the prevailing circumstances Norway could best serve this end by contributing to the work of the United Nations and by assuring that Norway did not become a political and military vacuum.[45] With regard to the latter task the Foreign Minister asked,

Is this a problem which Norway can solve alone or . . . can it only be solved in cooperation with others. And the next question which arises is "with whom?" Can we solve the problem in cooperation only with the Scandinavian countries or must the cooperation be more broadly based.[46]

The Foreign Minister said that these were the questions that were to be answered by the Scandinavian Defense Commission's investigation, whose report would be ready by the beginning of

February. In short, he demonstrated once again his view of "military and political vacuums" as destabilizing and dangerous in times of tension, and the concomitant responsibility the government had to insure that Norway did not continue to be in such a vacuum.[47]

These views expressed by Lange received the support of the Storting, and the foreign policy of the government enjoyed wide support in the press. In view of the Scandinavian defense investigations that were taking place simultaneously, it is particularly interesting to note remarks in the Labor party news organ, which took a much stronger line with regard to the questions that Lange raised in his statement to the Storting. The paper rejected the policy of neutrality "which led to the shipwreck of 1940" (and the policy which had been advocated by Sweden since the war and during the Scandinavian defense discussions). The paper added, referring to the exchange of views in the Storting,

The debate showed that there exists doubt as to the value of an isolated defense cooperation, or more correctly a Northern cooperation isolating Norway from lands to the West. . . . It must be clear to all that Norwegian public opinion makes it absolutely impossible to extend the Swedish neutrality policy to include Norway as well.[48]

It is clear that little modification of the strategic image of Norway had occurred since the spring re-evaluation that had marked the end of the policy of bridgebuilding. International tensions had undermined the possibilities for making the UN function as an instrument of international security, even though its other functions were important and should be supported. The Norwegian goal orientation was unmodified. Norway was searching for security in the event of war, looking for an arrangement that would maximize the possibilities of precluding "another 1940." Norway's "historical experience" was frequently mentioned in Norwegian policy statements and seemed to refer to the necessity to provide for defense in peace in order to help prevent war as well as to the strategic vulnerability of Norway.

Norway continued to perceive her geographic location as "strategic" and "exposed," leading to the judgment that Norway had little opportunity to remain aloof from another war should it occur. The Norwegian image of the structure of the system was somewhat modified with the Foreign Minister speaking often in terms of the Eastern and Western "blocs." Most spectacular was the refinement (not modification) of the process image which took place during the fall and winter of 1948. The Foreign Minister's fuzzy perception of the danger to world peace of undefended, strategically located areas became in the fall an unequivocal assertion that the primary danger to world peace was the existence of political and military vacuums. In other words, war was not viewed as a specified threat from one or another country or bloc, nor was it viewed as a consequence of one or another state's aggressive tendencies, but rather as an event that might occur as a result of the convergence of political tensions in areas of political instability and military vacuum.

Thus, unlike the Swedes *the Norwegian leadership did not perceive an inconsistency between bloc-building and international stability.* Rather the action response for Norway was obvious to both the Foreign Minister and the Prime Minister: insure domestically that Norway complete its reconstruction program in order to maintain political stability and take steps internationally to provide adequate defense arrangements. The judgment had already been made that Norway could not provide "adequate" defense unilaterally; thus, as the Norwegian Foreign Minister had stated, the question became "with whom does Norway collaborate?" In order to answer these questions, the Scandinavian defense investigations had been instituted, notwithstanding the fact that the "with whom" was not an open question for the Swedes as it was for the Norwegians.*

In short the Norwegian image of process looked to the creation of competing centers of political, economic, and military

---

* While the role played by economic considerations during this period were certainly important, the findings generated by this study (discussed in the final chapter) suggest they were not decisive. As the subsequent analysis indicates, the question of international collaboration appears to have been clearly decided with reference *primarily* to political and strategic (and not economic) considerations.

viability on which mutual trust and confidence could be built in order that the United Nations could perhaps be made to function as a security organization. Fortunately, Norwegian long-run aims regarding the United Nations were not inconsistent with the requirements imposed by her short-run aims: physical security in the event of war, the "unexpected and unpremeditated explosion," was consistent with strengthening the basis for great power collaboration in the United Nations.

The period of the Scandinavian political negotiations.—During the period of the Scandinavian defense investigations, political events continued to move at a faster pace both within and outside Scandinavia. The uncertainty on the American political scene, and especially with regard to U.S. foreign policy, was removed by the unexpected victory of President Truman in November, 1948, and late in the same month a preliminary draft of the North Atlantic pact was completed. On the Scandinavian scene the Scandinavian Defense Commission had met twice,[49] and because of the speed with which other options to Norway were presenting themselves,[50] it was decided on Norwegian initiative to hasten the completion of the work of the Defense Commission and to begin the political discussions of the possibilities of a Scandinavian defense arrangement even before the final report of the Commission was presented to the governments.

During its final meeting in Oslo in the middle of January the Scandinavian Defense Commission made its findings known to the governments. Its conclusions stated *inter alia*: (1) military co-operation among the three countries would strengthen their total defense capability; (2) the defenses of Norway and Denmark were insufficient and required considerable beefing up; (3) external material aid, on reasonable terms, was essential if the alliance was to be effective; Sweden could not deliver the military hardware that was required; (4) external military aid would be required in the event an attack on Scandinavia should take place.[51] Thus what began as purely "technical" discussions rapidly brought to a head the central political problem: what was to be the relationship between a Scandinavian defense bloc and the Western powers?

The political discussions among the Scandinavian governments commenced after the turn of the year in Karlstad,[52] Copenhagen,[53] and in Oslo.[54]

Prior to the Karlstad meeting all the principal actors on the Norwegian side made important foreign policy statements in the form of New Year's messages to the Norwegian people. The Prime Minister said that Norway must make every effort to find a common policy for Scandinavia to deal with the dangers that can threaten peace and freedom, and he also declared that Norway had an obligation to make a contribution to the larger responsibility that rests with all the Western European countries.[55]

Two days later the Foreign Minister repeated that though he did not think that any of the great powers was planning aggression, the tensions that prevailed in the world made possible the unwanted and unplanned "explosion." He then stated, indicating more explicitly than ever in the past, a new criterion for foreign policy choices.

Intensified great power tensions have made it more necessary than ever before that we be conscious of with whom we belong.[56]

The Foreign Minister said that these circumstances were forcing Norway to strengthen its security

through cooperation with countries which have the same political institutions as ourselves, a similar concept of democracy, and which live under somewhat homogeneous economic circumstances.

While this formulation did not exclude co-operation with Scandinavia,[57] Lange also made it explicit that he was not limiting himself to Scandinavia, reasoning,

But the more we consider these questions the more we will discover that we must find a way of expanding cooperation with peoples with whom we feel a kindred relationship, peoples outside the boundaries of Scandinavia, if we are to have full advantage of modern techniques and the possibilities they offer.[58]

The Foreign Minister then declared, implying that certain policy judgments had already been made on the Norwegian side, that

We must hope that Denmark and Sweden will come to these same conclusions so that we may stand together within the broader co-operation which is pending just as we now work together for the economic rehabilitation of Europe.

On the same day the Defense Minister made a statement which, although not revealing of Norwegian strategic thinking, should be noted because it was made so close to the opening of the political negotiations. Discussing the high costs of Norwegian defense and predicting that they would continue regardless of the political choices that might be made regarding the basis of Norwegian security policy, he suggested that

there is no reason to assume that participation in a larger security system which contains larger and richer powers would be the cheapest.[59]

The Defense Minister then declared that it was economically most reasonable and effective to "seek security through cooperation in a comprehensive security system which includes countries with greater resources and production capability than we have." In any case, the Defense Minister said, it was certain that in the absence of outside aid either (1) the time period for reconstruction would have to be extended or (2) the defense program would have to be reduced.

Thus even before the political negotiations began, the Norwegians were hardly speaking as if they shared the views of the Swedes. The Prime Minister talked of "dangers" and "threats" to the peace, perceptions that were not shared by the Swedes; the Foreign Minister indicated that a policy decision had already been made (albeit with the hope that Sweden and Denmark would "come to the same conclusions"); and if the policy decision had indeed not been made, the Defense Minister indirectly suggested that, at least in terms of the economic implications, it might be a good idea to make it!

The first of the Scandinavian defense pact negotiations opened several days later in Karlstad and was attended by the Prime Ministers, Foreign Ministers, and Defense Ministers of the three countries. Although the communiqué issued following the conclusion of the meeting was not very revealing, it is known that a fairly comprehensive proposal was considered by the parties. The "Karlstad Plan" acknowledged the efficacy of a Scandinavian defense alliance, noted the desirability of Norway and Denmark's obtaining arms supplies from outside Scandinavia, limited the operation of the alliance to the Scandinavian area proper (i.e., Greenland, Svalbard, and the Faeroes would not be included), and established the principle of "freedom from alliances" as the political basis of the proposed pact.[60]

Thus were raised the two issues that were to dominate the political discussions: (1) the question of the military capability of the proposed alliance, and (2) the question of the political orientation of the alliance.

With regard to the first question, Sweden had made it a condition on her side that Denmark and Norway should initiate a rearmament program on a substantial scale in order to bring their defense capability up to a level more comparable with Sweden's. This condition immediately raised the question of military supplies and created an issue between the Swedes and the Norwegians with regard to external aid, for it could not be questioned that Norway and Denmark would encounter great difficulties in attempting to undertake a comprehensive rearmament program on their own.

Because the Swedes, on the other hand, were unable to provide sufficient material aid to the Norwegians and the Danes making possible such rearmament, by the first Karlstad meeting the Swedes had accepted the idea of external military aid, and by the second meeting at Copenhagen the Swedes, like the Norwegians and the Danes, made it a condition for their participation in the alliances that Norway and Denmark obtain equipment and other forms of military assistance from the Western powers in order to complete the reconstruction of their defenses. By the time of the final Oslo meeting however, where the negotiations for a Scandinavian defense alliance finally failed, the Swedes were prepared to drop deliveries of Western armaments as a condition of their participation; the Norwegians, however, continued to insist that such aid was absolutely essential and this was accepted by Sweden, but the issue of arms supplies was not explicitly raised at Oslo because the discussions were dominated by political questions.

Thus the separate but related rearmament and arms supply issues can be summarized as follows: Sweden at all times made it a condition of her participation in the proposed defense alliance that Norway and Denmark should rearm on a substantial scale. By the time of the meeting at Copenhagen both the Swedes and the Norwegians regarded arms deliveries from the West, and particularly from the United States, as a mutually accepted condition. Later at the Oslo meeting, Sweden was willing to relinquish American aid as a condition of her participation, but the entire question of military supplies had already brought to the surface the overriding political question. Thus the opportunity did not exist for the Swedes to bring to the attention of the Norwegians the modification of their position regarding military aid because of the essential divergence regarding the political character of the proposed association.[61]

With regard to the question of the political character of the proposed alliance, the Swedes continued to assert their unchanging view that a Scandinavian defense arrangement ought to be formally and unequivocally a league of armed neutrality;[62] any co-operation with the great powers in military matters was to be strictly prohibited. The Norwegians, on the other hand, felt that the Scandinavian bloc could not isolate itself from the West, *especially* with regard to military matters. That Sweden had agreed to Norway's receiving military aid from the West represented a major concession on her part, and although it was later charged in Norway that the government had not taken advantage of this concession by the Swedish government, it seems obvious that the *political* differences were crucial, and *only* their solution by agreement would have placed the question of defense supplies in a central position with regard to the ultimate outcome of the negotiations.

With regard then to the political issues, the next major statement on the Norwegian side that should be noted came in a report to the Storting by the Foreign Minister on the Copenhagen meeting. Lange noted that "under certain circumstances" a possibility existed for reaching a mutually binding but otherwise isolated Scandinavian defense alliance." [63] In this regard the Foreign Minister declared that at Karlstad both the Norwegians and the Swedes had made great concessions: the Swedes were willing to modify their policy of non-alliances in favor of an alliance with Norway and Denmark, and the Norwegians made "substantial concessions" regarding

the principal Norwegian view that we are willing, if the prerequisites are otherwise present, to accept a Scandinavian defense alliance without a formal tie to a larger regional security system. . . .[64]

He then went on to point out that the Scandinavian Defense Commission had concluded that a Scandinavian alliance would not possess the economic capability to provide sufficient military supplies from within and that a Scandinavian alliance would also require "military assistance in the event that one or more of the countries in the alliance were attacked." Lange said this led to the discussion of the more deep-rooted differences in the views among the three countries, differences that the communiqué following the Copenhagen meeting referred to as the "prerequisites for and consequences of the alliance-free pact." Thus the negotiators found themselves locked once again on the political question, what Lange referred to as the "character of the pact."

Lange then declared once again his now well-established view regarding the reasons for the different evaluations made by the three countries.

Our security problems, in part because of the dissimilarities in our geographic situation, are not identical. During the last war our people have had entirely different historical experiences. The genuine differences in these two areas have led to the difference in our views of the central problems of our foreign and security policies.[65]

Lange then proceeded to state again the Norwegian view of the current problem in international politics, declaring that

We can best render our contribution to the stabilization of our part of the world, and thereby the peace of the world, on the basis of a concept of the solidarity among the democratic peoples and of joint regional cooperation within an area which is sufficiently large to represent a bona fide power factor.

Thus is revealed once again Lange's view that the building of blocs under the circumstances would be a stabilizing factor in world politics. Lange clearly felt that stability in Northern Europe would contribute directly to the creation of general international stability, and, further, that stability in Northern Europe could best be effected by its participation in a wider regional arrangement that would possess a more formidable potential for influence. Lange then added what is perhaps his most revealing statement of his view of the role of a Scandinavian bloc and thus his purpose in the Scandinavian defense negotiations.

It is therefore our view that an isolated defense pact among Denmark, Norway, and Sweden, even in the absence of a formal tie to a greater security system, in its character and its substance must build on this more comprehensive concept of security.

Lange added further that if such were the basis of the Scandinavian alliance, only then could it hope for the political and material support of the leading democratic powers. On the other hand, the Foreign Minister declared this view was not shared by the Swedes. He said that the spokesmen for the Swedes in Copenhagen were adamant that the proposed pact "must be genuinely alliance-free and not in any form rely on the concept of a security policy of regional solidarity outside the borders of the three participating countries." [66]

Because of the differences in political views, it was decided to conclude the meeting in Copenhagen and try again in Oslo at a later date, providing the opportunity for additional consultations between the governments and the political parties in each of the countries. Lange stated, however, that all parties agreed that the establishment of a defense alliance that included nations with excessively dissimilar views of the central problems of foreign policy and of the best means to employ to reach the common goal of securing peace would be unjustifiable and would dissolve with the first serious crisis. Nevertheless the Oslo meeting would be held to determine whether a common political basis for the Scandinavian defense alliance could be found, but, as has been pointed out, the Oslo meeting failed to produce agreement.[67]

After the failure in Oslo, the Norwegian Prime Minister said that if only good will had been sufficient to reach agreement, a Scandinavian defense pact would exist, but that the failure was a result of more fundamental causes, declaring that

the reasons the discussions today did not lead to a positive result is that our security problems are inherently different, or that in any case today we evaluate them differently.[68]

The move toward the Atlantic Pact.—Several days following the failure of the Scandinavian defense negotiations, the Norwegian Foreign Minister reported to the Storting. He provided another of his general reviews of the course of events since the end of the war, noting that the failure of the UN as a security instrument forced all countries, including Norway, to look to regional security arrangements.[69] Before providing his colleagues with an explanation of the reasons for the failure of the negotiations, the Foreign Minister noted what he considered to be the two salient problems in Norwegian security policy. They were

Norway is not and can never become on its own sufficiently strong militarily

(a) to deter a great power from making an attack on the country or

(b) to repel a great power's attack.[70]

For these reasons the Foreign Minister suggested that Norway must find a policy that would insure for itself *by advance agreement* military assistance from other states both to preserve peace and for immediate aid in the event of war.

Lange then declared that the second important problem was related to the question of external assistance.

> In order to be able to build up the defense of the country we must have supplies of weapons and other military provisions from abroad.[71]

Lange then cited the geographic position of Norway, and its Western democratic values, suggesting that since the country was being forced to seek security through closer associations with other states rather than through the United Nations, "it is self-evident that we must seek such cooperation more or less within the framework of this democratic circle of states."[72] For this reason Norway had decided to discuss these problems first with her Scandinavian neighbors.

After providing a long account of the negotiations, the Foreign Minister declared that they failed because of (1) the inability of the Swedes and the Norwegians to agree on the political character of the alliance, (2) their different views as to the best means of preventing war, and (3) the low probability, in view of Western policy, of obtaining the necessary deliveries of military supplies.[73]

The Foreign Minister also noted in his speech that Norway had been approached by the Americans and the British concerning Norway's inclusion in the discussions on the proposed Atlantic Pact.[74] At the time of the approach, however, Lange said Norway wished to explore in greater detail the possibility of a Scandinavian arrangement.

At the conclusion of his speech he declared that the three Scandinavian countries must now attempt on their own to solve their individual security problems. He assured his colleagues that Norway had not yet received, nor had it requested, a formal invitation to join the Atlantic discussions. The Foreign Minister asserted that more information was required before a position could be taken by the government and debated by the Storting.

If it appeared to many in the Storting that Norway, notwithstanding Lange's "need for more information," was about to join in the Atlantic Pact discussions, it also was of concern to the Soviet Union, for in the period between the beginning of the abortive Oslo meeting and the Foreign Minister's statement to the Storting, the Norwegians and the Soviets had had, on Soviet initiative, a significant diplomatic exchange.[75]

A stern but polite Soviet note asserted that the Atlantic Pact represented a group of powers pursuing aggressive aims, including the establishment of air and naval bases on the periphery of the Soviet Union. It reminded the government of Norway's common frontier with the U.S.S.R. and requested to be informed of the Norwegian attitude toward the Atlantic Pact, whether reports of its intention to join were true, and whether obligations had been undertaken for the establishment of air or naval bases on Norwegian territory.[76]

The prompt Norwegian reply was remarkably calm, especially in view of the impact that the Soviet note had made in Norway and in the West. The Norwegians noted the failure of the UN as a security instrument and stated that Norway was convinced that "it is necessary to seek increased security through regional defense cooperation." The Norwegians established the failure of the Scandinavian negotiations and noted that they would

> make a closer investigation into the forms of, and under what conditions Norway might be able to take part in, a regional security system comprising the countries around the Atlantic.[77]

The Norwegian note then made an important commitment to the Soviets with regard to their future freedom of action. Noting the long period of peaceful relations between the two countries,

> the Norwegian asks the Soviet Government to be assured that Norway will never take part in a policy with aggressive aims. She will never allow Norwegian territory to be used in the service of such a policy. *The Norwegian Government will not* join in any agreement

with other States involving obligations to *open bases for the military forces of foreign Powers on Norwegian territory as long as Norway is not attacked or exposed to threats of* attack.[78]

Here is encountered the genesis of the so-called Norwegian *base policy*. Although the base policy is not within the scope of this inquiry, it is unquestionably a manifestation in a concrete situation of the deep-rooted Norwegian sensitivity to Soviet security interests. It can also be said in passing that if the Norwegian government was attempting to assure the Soviets that they had nothing to fear in the event that Norway joined the Atlantic Pact, it was also attempting to reassure elements in its own domestic public that were strongly opposed to the stationing of foreign troops on Norwegian soil.[79] One other factor of some importance that was undoubtedly operational in the base policy commitment is Norwegian concern for the fate of Finland under the terms of the 1948 Treaty, especially if the Soviets perceived a "provocation." [80]

The Soviets replied several days later [81] that the Norwegian government's position regarding bases was "insufficient" and proceeded to offer the Norwegians a non-aggression pact, reminding them again of their mutual boundary.

The Norwegian reply to the Soviet *démarche* however, was delayed for a month, for on the same day as the delivery of the Soviet note the Norwegian Foreign Minister headed a delegation to Washington and London to make, as he had suggested in his last address to the Storting, further inquiry concerning the nature of the proposed Atlantic Pact.[82]

The next major statement of the Norwegian position did not come until Lange's report to the National Convention of the Labor party on the international situation, implying that Norway was on the threshold of an historic decision. Although the speech provided another general review of international events followed by a plea by the Prime Minister for the Convention to take a stand on the question of the future course of Norwegian foreign policy,[83] several points made by the Foreign Minister should be noted.

First, in view of the still unanswered Soviet offer of a non-aggression pact and the continuing crisis in Berlin, the Foreign Minister's view of the Soviet Union was remarkably consistent. Although the Foreign Minister said that the Soviets were primarily responsible for the paralysis of the United Nations [84] and hindered other attempts toward creative international cooperation,[85] he said he had "no intention of one-sidedly citing the Russians as the bogey in international politics." [86] The Foreign Minister said that the Russians alone did not bear the responsibility for the course of events after the war.

I am fully aware that there have been errors and serious errors also by the Western great powers. I am also aware that the Russians have good reasons for their suspicions of the Western countries [87]

In spite of this, and notwithstanding the aid from, and good faith demonstrated by, the Russians during the liberation of North Norway, the Soviet's diplomatic and political offensive in Eastern Europe was cited by Lange as mainly responsible for the international tensions that existed and which therefore was forcing Norway to look to regional security arrangements.[88] Nevertheless the Foreign Minister did not say that Norway was threatened directly by Soviet aggression, but persisted in his view that

No great power today desires to start a world war; on the other hand it is also evident that danger is to be found in an unwanted and unintentional war occurring anyway.

Because of this danger of an unpremeditated war and because the security apparatus of the United Nations could not function, Norway turned to a consideration of regional arrangements: first to Scandinavia and then to the evolving Western alliance. In discussing these actions, Lange clearly revealed his assumptions and reasons for his foreign policy goals.

After the alternative of a non-committed Scandinavian association had been dropped, it was essential that our standpoint should be clear. In view of the tension in the international situation, we cannot allow Norway to lie militarily impotent and open to attack. To allow Norway to continue to be a military and political vacuum increases not only the risks for ourselves, but it also helps to increase the uncertainty of the entire international situation, and it therefore contrary to that which is the main aim of our entire policy in the international sphere.

The Foreign Minister said that the real need was to create "a power sufficiently strong to deter all from attack," and in this regard it was obvious that neither Norway nor Scandinavia was sufficiently large to take full advantage of modern military and economic techniques.[89]

It was clear that the Norwegian government had two preferred outcomes: to deter war and to insure in advance external aid should war occur. Further, one policy was viewed as consistently serving both of these aims: a regional approach to international collaboration based on some form of "understanding" with the Western powers. And now that the Scandinavian defense pact discussions had failed, it could be anticipated that the "understanding" would be explicit in the form of Norwegian membership in the Atlantic alliance. In the view of the government,

A weak Norway without allies is a danger—not only for our own peace, but for the peace of the world.[90]

On the other hand, a policy which would result in a Norway

which has rebuilt its defense and which is solidly anchored in cooperation with other democratic countries can render a contribution not only to ensure its own security, but also to stabilize and strengthen the democratic world and thereby world peace.

Thus if the great danger to world peace was inadequately defended but strategically important real estate encouraging an unintended war, the best way to deter such a war was to establish in advance a clear-cut, mutually binding commitment among the Western democracies.

The National Convention of the Labor party finally adopted a resolution which concluded that Norway must solve its security problems in joint and binding collaboration with the Western democracies in the area of defense policy.[91]

Following this endorsement, the government went to the Storting to request permission to join the preparatory discussions on the North Atlantic Pact so that Norway might be able to assert her views before the Pact was completed.[92] In this statement, the Foreign Minister repeated all the major arguments and reasons that had forced Norway to look to regional security arrangements. He emphasized the need to prevent war by "shaping a new stability" within the framework of a "real power factor in world politics," noting that

A solidarity which is limited to small entities which are otherwise neutral cannot have the effect necessary to prevent war.[93]

The Foreign Minister also said that the Scandinavian alliance was not "a practical political possibility." Not only was it not so for the reason suggested above, but also for a more fundamental reason,

It is not consistent with the solidarity in relation to the democracies in Western Europe and North America, which we *during the entire period of the Scandinavian defense negotiations thought necessary to secure peace.*[94]

Lange noted for his colleagues that although Norway was required to make a choice, no pressure would be exerted by the West for Norway to choose the Atlantic Pact, telling them at the same time that he favored joining the discussions and reminding them of the unanswered Soviet offer of a non-aggression pact, saying that the government would not reply until the Storting had taken a position on the Atlantic Pact discussions.[95]

Early in March the Storting met in secret session and agreed to Norway's joining the final round of discussions on the Atlantic Pact against the eleven votes of the Communists after defeating a Communist motion to accept the proffered non-aggression pact.[96] On the same day the government replied to the Soviet note, citing the UN Charter and politely rejecting the non-aggression pact as redundant, and announced its intention to join the Atlantic Pact discussions, recognizing at the same time the long history of good neighborly relations, adding the Norwegian desire to preserve them, and reaffirming the Norwegian base declaration.[97]

On the following day a public debate was held in the Storting on the Foreign Minister's February statement on the question of Norway's participation in the Atlantic Pact discussions.[98]

Later in the month the government drafted a bill to sanction Norwegian accession to the Atlantic Pact,[99] and this was presented to the Storting for its approval on March 29, 1949. After an extended debate,[100] which was almost a carbon copy of the preceding major foreign policy debate, the Storting sanctioned Norway's signing and ratification of the Atlantic Pact by a vote of 130 to 13. The dissenters included the eleven Communist members plus two dissident members of the Labor party.[101]

Finally on April 4, 1949, Foreign Minister Lange signed the North Atlantic Treaty in Washington making Norway one of the twelve charter members of the North Atlantic Alliance.

1. At the risk of redundancy, it seems appropriate to emphasize again, especially in view of all that has been said about "Norway's return to neutrality" after the war, the seriousness of the Norwegian view of the security functions of the UN. The UN was more than a "good thing"; it was an instrument created, in part, to preserve peace in a world where force counted a great deal, and the Norwegians refused to doubt that their concerted efforts to make it succeed would fail.

2. It will be recalled that the Foreign Minister had as early as January, 1948, recognized the essential weaknesses of and contradictions within the United Nations; however (to the discomfort of many in Norway who did not share his evaluation), he unequivocally reaffirmed the policy of bridgebuilding. Thus paralysis in the United Nations could be tolerated as long as Norway was not perceived as threatened. It is interesting to note that the Norwegians could have hypothetically tolerated a threat to their security if the UN's security functions were perceived as effective.

3. Reference here to the "Soviet Union" and the "Western bloc" is in recognition of the fact that the so-called "Eastern bloc" was in reality a series of bilateral agreements with the Soviet Union and was not a multilateral "bloc" until May, 1955, with the signing of the Warsaw Pact. The Western bloc, however, was based from the beginning on multilateral agreements.

4. Revision would especially be required in her image of process and her image of geographic location.

5. However, Lange's formulation left no reason to believe that Norway was committed to a Scandinavian orientation as an alternative to the United Nations. In fact, quite the opposite is implied: under certain circumstances Norway might be compelled to opt for a policy different from Denmark or Sweden since different problems are often not susceptible of common solutions.

6. The plans were presented to the Council on April 23–24, 1948. For an excellent and exhaustive chronological account of the public statements of the three major actors in the Scandinavian defense negotiations and discussions from January, 1948, to April, 1949, see Barbara Haskel, "Forsøket på å skape et Skandinavisk forsvarsforbund," *Internasjonal Politikk*, II (1965), pp. 91–131.

7. Foreign Minister Undén was in Oslo on May 3, 1948. See Wilhelm Keilhau, "Norway and the Atlantic Pact," *Norseman*, Vol. VII (March–April, 1949).

8. This date was the occasion of the National Convention of the Social Democrats in Sweden which was attended by Danish Prime Minister Hedtoft and Norwegian Prime Minister Gerhardsen. The latter, in an address to the delegates, stated that "the question of cooperation in the military field has been lately raised in different quarters. We ought perhaps to examine whether there exists a basis for such cooperation." See Sveriges Socialdemokratiska Arbetarpartis Kongress, *Protokoll*, May 9–14, 1948, pp. 17–18. Swedish Prime Minister Erlander said, "It is an urgent task to examine whether the confidence, friendship, and trust can become the basis for a practical cooperation," although difficulties which could not be underestimated would have to be overcome. Hedtoft said that co-operation was necessary because a threat to one country in Scandinavia was a threat to all of them.

9. The lecture was delivered on June 4, 1948. Halvard Lange, *Norsk Utenrikspolitikk siden 1945* (Oslo: Johan Grundt Tanum, 1952), p. 69.

10. *Ibid.* Lange said in this regard that "the defensive ability which a co-ordinated defense would represent would exceed the arithmetic sum of the three countries' defenses." Lange, it should be noted, always, spoke on terms of "defense coordination" or "cooperation" and never in terms of a "pact" or an "alliance." This becomes even more significant in retrospect, since it is known that the Swedes were, at least privately, speaking in these latter terms.

11. *Ibid.*, pp. 69–70.

12. *Ibid.*, p. 70. The following day, June 5, 1948, Lange said in a speech in Copenhagen that "we in Norway consider that the development of the military technique during and since the last war has put us, strategically speaking, in a very exposed position. We therefore think it right to recognize realistically that the possibility of keeping our country out of any future war is not particularly great." Cited in the *Norseman*, VI (July–August, 1948), 254.

13. On the general subject of Danish foreign policy during this period the best capsule summary can be found in Erik Reske-Nielsen and Erik Kragh, *Atlantpagten og Danmark 1949–62* (København: Atlantsammenslutningen, 1962), chap. i, "Vejen Til Atlantpagten," especially pp. 26–48; for a summary in English see Sven Henningsen, "The Foreign Policy of Denmark,"

in Joseph E. Black and Kenneth W. Thompson, *Foreign Policies in a World of Change* (New York: Harper & Row, 1963), pp. 100–103.

14. The statement was made by Foreign Minister Rasmussen on June 2, 1948, two days prior to Lange's Malmö address, in a foreign policy debate in the lower house (Folketing) of the Rigsdag. Cited in G. Naesselund Hansen, "Current Problems in Danish Foreign Policy," *Norseman,* VI (July–August, 1948), 217.

15. Reference here is to Hans Hedtoft. The "Scandinavianism" of the Prime Minister is discussed in Carlo Christensen, "Hans Hedtoft," *American Scandinavian Review,* XLIII (June, 1955), 136–40.

16. On this see Hans Engen, "Disagreement in the North," *Norseman,* VI (July–August, 1948), 213, who argued, "Denmark cannot be defended . . . Discussions concerning a Northern Alliance should therefore in reality be confined to Norway and Sweden." See also Franklin Scott, *The United States and Scandinavia* (Cambridge: Harvard University Press, 1950), p. 308.

17. See Haskel, *op. cit.*

18. An articulate activist element advocating greater Swedish involvement in international politics has long existed in Sweden, although it has never been able to obtain widespread public support or influence decisively government policy. Nevertheless Sweden has had many close calls: in the Crimean War and the Schleswig-Holstein crisis in the nineteenth century, and in the twentieth century during the Union crisis of 1905 and on behalf of Finland both in World War I and World War II. See Herbert Tingsten, "Issues in Swedish Foreign Policy," *Foreign Affairs,* XXXVII (April, 1959), 474. Tingsten, the editor of *Dagens Nyheter,* is a modern activist, having long been a leading proponent of Swedish membership in the Atlantic alliance.

19. See Karl Birnbaum, *Swedish Foreign Policy* (Stockholm: The Swedish Institute, 1962), pp. 1–5; and Charles O. Lerche, Jr., "Sweden: Neutralism or Neutrality?" *U.S. Naval Institute Proceedings,* LXXXVII (January, 1961), 68–75.

20. See Rowland Kenney, *The Northern Tangle* (London: J. M. Dent, 1946), pp. 221–22.

21. The great appeal and almost unquestioned efficacy of the non-alliance policy which is often said to exist among the Swedes is given strong expression in Åke Sandler, "Sweden's Post-War Diplomacy: Some Problems, Views, and Issues," *Western Political Quarterly,* CXXXI (December, 1960), 924–33. See also Nils Andrén and Åke Landqvist, *Svensk Utrikespolitik efter Krigen* (Stockholm: Almqvist & Wiksell, 1965).

22. Reske-Nielsen and Kragh, *op. cit.,* pp. 45–47; Sandler, *op. cit.,* p. 184.

23. Undén made this statement in a speech to the Social Democrats' National Convention on May 11, 1948. See Sveriges Socialdemokratiska Arbetarpartis Kongress, *Protokoll,* p. 124.

24. On this point see Tingsten, *op. cit.,* p. 475; and Sandler, *op. cit.,* pp. 179, 184.

25. Swedish Defense Minister Vough quoted in *Stockholms Tidingen,* April 27, 1948 (editorial). See also Gunnar Hägglöf, *A Test of Neutrality* (Stockholm: The Swedish Institute, 1961), pp. 21–22, who cites the military posture of Sweden (in addition to broad domestic political support and the

"balance of power") as an important factor in her defense of neutrality in World War II; and Birnbaum, *op. cit.,* p. 4.

26. See on this Gunnar Heckscher, *Sweden and the East-West Conflict* (Stockholm: The Swedish Institute, 1961), p. 4; and Sandler, *op. cit.,* p. 184.

27. The meeting was held in Stockholm on September 8–9, 1948.

28. Reference here is to Senate Resolution 239, June 11, 1948, reported in *Department of State Bulletin,* XIX (July 18, 1948), 79–80.

29. Negotiations opened on July 6, 1948.

30. Hans Engen, "Disagreement in the North," *Norseman,* VI (July–August, 1948), 213. Engen suggests that Swedish aloofness from great power blocs would be threatened if Norway or Denmark were associated with the great powers. "For this, in the opinion of the Swedish government, would undermine the foundations of Swedish neutrality policy. If Norway, for example, pledged itself to the West, the Soviet Union would no longer take seriously Sweden's ability to maintain its neutrality. It must be a primary task of the Swedish government to prevent Norway from pledging itself to the West. This presumably is the chief reason why the Swedish government is now favorably disposed to the idea of a Northern military alliance. It is an attempt to offer compensation to Norway for the security which it would otherwise seek in an agreement with the West."

31. *Viktige storpolitiske Dokumenter 1945–50,* (Bergen: Chr. Michelsens Institutt, 1950), pp. 89–90.

32. See the *Baltimore Sun,* September 10, 1948.

33. The meeting was held on October 15, 1948. For additional information see *News of Norway,* VI, No. 3 (October 23, 1948), 2. The members of the Commission were for Norway: Trygve Bratteli, Dag Bryn, W. Munthe Kaas, and Lt. General Ole Berg; for Denmark: Vice-Admiral A. H. Vedel, Frantz Hvass, Poul Hansen, and Harald Petersen; and for Sweden: Carl Hamilton, Elon Anderson, Sven Andersson (later replaced by G. F. Thapper), and Nils Swedlund.

34. The speech was before a blue-ribbon audience in Oslo on October 19, 1948, in honor of the Linge Company, the famous wartime underground group which sabotaged the Nazi's heavy water production at Rjukan. See *Morgenbladet,* October 20, 1948.

35. *Ibid.* It is interesting to note that following the war a special investigation commission was appointed to probe the actions of Norwegian officials preceding and following the German invasion. The report strongly criticized the defense policies of the Nygaardsvold government, held Foreign Minister Koht "negligent" in keeping the government informed, and sharply criticized Defense Minister Ljungberg for failing to strengthen Norwegian defenses until the night of the invasion. The major actors responded by demanding a trial before the Norwegian High Court. That the official charges of negligence and "too little too late" and the dramatic events that followed served as "lessons" to the postwar government has been suggested as a part of the so-called Ninth of April complex. *Norway Digest,* Vol. XLIX, December 6, 1946; and Vol. L, December 13, 1946.

36. *Stortingstidende,* "Regegjørelse fra utenriksministeren om den utenrikspolitiske situasjon," October 30, 1948.

37. *Ibid.,* p. 1984. Lange also noted that the continuing tension could lead to a "hysterical anticommunism in the West, tempting the democracies to cooperate openly with authoritarian regimes."

38. *Ibid.,* p. 1984–85. This "third image" view of war was especially pronounced in Lange's Military Society speech in April. For a provoking analysis of images of the "causes" of war, see Kenneth Waltz, *Man, the State, and War* (New York: Columbia University Press, 1959), *passim.*

39. Lange made specific reference here to the Indochina problem, Palestine, and Kashmir.

40. *Ibid.,* p. 1985. In this regard Lange mentioned the inability of the UN to establish international control over nuclear weapons. The failure he attributed directly to the refusal of the U.S.S.R. and the Eastern European states to accept any form of international control. This is worth noting for most of Lange's references to the Soviet Union (unlike this one) are presented as evaluations made by others rather than his own judgments.

41. *Ibid.,* p. 1986.

42. In a different context the Foreign Minister spoke of the "exposed strategic position Norway has today as a consequence of the development of air and war techniques." References to the evolution of "war techniques" and their transformation of Norway's strategic position can be traced back to the early 1940's, and they continued to be made frequently through the bridge-building period of Norwegian policy.

43. *Ibid.* Lange added, "Nevertheless it is clear that there is so much which binds us together that we must attempt to see if it is possible to overcome that which separates." In any case the scope of the investigations is apparently including both economic and military problems, and the nature of the investigations is to determine consequences of a Scandinavian defense arrangement for the security needs of each of the countries.

44. *Stortingstidende,* "Debatt om utenriksministerens redegjørelse 30 okt. og 6 desbr.," December 10, 1948, p. 2530.

45. *Ibid.,* p. 2533. Lange, in answer to criticism which suggested that he was short-sighted with regard to the danger of war, said "I have not said that we are confronted by an immediate danger of war. . . . But there are present at all times the possibilities of an unpremeditated explosion, and it is not defensible to close one's eyes to the anguish and uncertainty about what the near future can bring."

46. *Ibid.* Lange said there were limits, not far removed, to Norway's ability to defend herself without seriously threatening the program of reconstruction. Moreover this threshold should not be crossed in Lange's view for it would weaken the "defense will" of the people.

47. Although the Storting gave overwhelming support to the foreign policy of the government, it came under strong criticism from the Communists (who refused support) as well as from others (including some in the Labor party) who felt either that the government was not moving with sufficient speed to solve Norway's security problems or that the government was adopting an excessively negative attitude toward the possibilities of a Scandinavian defense arrangement. It should be noted that the government requested and the Storting provided another extraordinary defense appropriation on December 10, 1948, in excess of the 100 million kroner ($20 million) appropriated on March 16, 1948.

48. From *Arbeiderbladet,* cited in *News of Norway,* VI, No. 12 (December 25, 1948), 46.

49. The Defense Commission met November 15–17, 1948, in Saltsjöbaden, Sweden, and December 15–19 in Hornbaek, Denmark.

50. Tim Greve, *Norway and NATO* (Oslo: Norwegian Universities Press, 1963), p. 12, states that around the New Year of 1949 the Norwegian and Danish governments were "secretly informed that the two countries would be invited to join the Atlantic Pact . . . if they themselves wished to accept an invitation of this kind." Public references to the invitation to Denmark and Norway (not Sweden) can be found in the Oslo press on January 7, 1949. Lange himself said in February, 1949, that Norway was informed on December 24 that it could participate in the discussions on the Atlantic Pact. (He actually said " . . . one week after the meeting in Uddevalla . . . " and that reference was to a meeting on December 17, 1948.) See *Stortingstidende,* "Redegj. fra utenriksministeren om forhandl. om forsvarsforbund," February 3, 1949, p. 174.

51. Although the findings were not made public they were generally known. See Greve, *op. cit.,* pp. 11–12; Arne Skaug, "Hovedproblemer i norsk utenrikspolitikk," Lecture before the NATO Defense College, Paris, May 13, 1953 (Oslo: Utenriksmelding no. 60/1953); also see statements by Lange to the Storting cited in Utenriksdepartementets Presseteneste, *Norges Linje* (Oslo: Tiden, 1949), pp. 19, 28–29. (Hereinafter referred to as *Norges Linje.*)

52. January 5–6, 1949.

53. January 22–24, 1949. Representatives of the participating countries' parliaments attended.

54. January 29–30, 1949. For a chronological account of the various meetings see *Norges Linje,* pp. 1–2; for a chronological account of the discussions see Haskel, *op. cit.*

55. *Arbeiderbladet,* January 3, 1949. It should be noted that the Norwegian perception of "dangers" which can threaten the peace (i.e., politico-military vacuums) were not the same "dangers" perceived by the Swedes.

56. *Arbeiderbladet,* January 3, 1949.

57. Lange said, "It is natural for us that we should first determine to what degree we can strengthen ourselves by extending in all fields our cooperation with Denmark, Sweden, and Iceland, and with Finland in certain areas."

58. *Arbeiderbladet,* January 3, 1949.

59. *Ibid.*

60. See on this Wilfred Ryder, "The End of Nordic Neutrality," *Soundings,* XXIV (March, 1949), 20; on Greenland and Iceland see an article in *Fedrelandsvennen,* January 15, 1949; see also *Morgenbladet,* February 10, 1949, reporting on statements made from the Swedish side.

61. This account of the course of events is *post facto* information not available at the time of the negotiations and is extracted largely from an article written collectively by Prime Minister Gerhardsen, Defense Minister Hauge (at the time of the writing both were retired), and Foreign Minister Lange in *Arbeiderbladet,* January 8, 1952. The above discussion has only peripheral relevance to the evolution and application of the Norwegian strategic image

and is included here only because the question of defense supplies has been central to most discussions of this period in both Swedish and Norwegian foreign policies. The statement by the three primary Norwegian actors was prompted by a critical article appearing in *Kontakt* magazine (a vehicle of left-wing Labor party views at the time): Johanne Åmlid, "Hvilke betingelser stilte Sverige under de nordiske forsvarsforhandlinger?", V (December, 1951), 1, 40, 41, which charged, in effect, that the Norwegian government had missed the opportunity for Scandinavian co-operation in defense matters by "misunderstanding" just what it was the Swedes were establishing as "conditions." Åmlid's article contains reference to and quotes from an interesting personal letter from Swedish Prime Minister Erlander which argues that the Swedes had not made arms deliveries from the *U.S.* a condition, but which does not deny that Norway and Denmark were to be rearmed. Thus it seems rather a moot point to argue about "conditions," for the Swedes *did* require rearmament and the Norwegians made the judgment that such rearmament could not be effected without external aid. Therefore the Swedish demand for rearmament became in effect, as a result of Norwegian economic judgments, a demand for Western military supplies. Erlander's views regarding the debate were stated in January, 1952, and reported in Royal Ministry of Foreign Affairs, *Documents on Swedish Foreign Policy 1952* (Stockholm: Kungl-Boktryckeriet, 1957), pp. 7–9; Erlander's views were clearly stated following the failure of the negotiations when he was invited to speak before the Norwegian Labor Party National Convention. See the Norsk Arbeiderparti, *Landsmøtet 1949 Protokoll* (Oslo: Arbeidernes Aktietrykkeri, 1950), pp. 174–76. (Hereinafter cited as *Protokoll*.)

62. In fact two days prior to the second round of the negotiations in Copenhagen, Swedish Foreign Minister Undén provided one of the most explicit formulations of the Swedish position in a Riksdag debate, speaking of a binding Scandinavian defense alliance, based on neutrality, standing outside of great power groupings in times of peace, and aiming toward non-involvement in the event of war. Undén's statement is quoted in Haskel, *op. cit.*, and was referred to by Foreign Minister Lange in his statement to the Storting at the end of January, 1949. See *Norges Linje*, p. 21 or *Stortingstidende*, "Redegj. fra utenriksministeren om Københavnforhandlinger," January 27, 1949, p. 134.

63. *Norges Linje*, pp. 18–19. (This and the following citations can be found also in "Redegj. fra utenriksministeren om Københavnforhandlinger," *Stortingtidende*, January 27, 1949, pp. 133–35.)

64. *Ibid.*, p. 19.

65. *Ibid.*, p. 20.

66. *Ibid.*, p. 21. It is interesting to note the addition of italics in the reprinting of the Foreign Minister's statement in *Norges Linje* from *Stortingstidende*. The word "character" previously mentioned in connection with the discussion of the political orientation of the alliance is italicized in the reprinting. Similarly italics have been added to the word "it" in Norwegian, which, as a result of the Norwegian syntax, makes unmistakable Lange's point regarding the necessity of rooting a Scandinavian alliance in a more comprehensive security system.

67. The communiqué stated *inter alia* that "discussions have now revealed that for the present it is not possible to reach the necessary concordance as to the prerequisites for, and consequences of, the alliance-free defense league

which has been under discussion. Therefore, there is insufficient basis for entry into such a mutually binding league at the present time." Cited in *News of Norway*, VI (February 5, 1949), 65.

68. "Statsminister Gerhardsens tale ved avslutningen av Oslomøtet 30 januar 1949," *Norges Linje*, pp. 34–35.

69. The speech was made on February 3, 1949. Lange said, "But the developments in the outside world have forced us to reconsider our security policy." See *Stortingstidende*, "Redegj. fra utenriksministeren om forhandl. om forsvarsforbund," February, 1949, pp. 172–76, with the debate following, pp. 176–97; also reported in *Norges Linje*, p. 25.

70. *Norges Linje*, p. 26. It should be noted that point "a" represents one of the major judgments of the Norwegians that was not shared by the Swedes. The Swedes felt that their experience in World War II indicated the deterrence value of a relatively small but solid and alert defense establishment. (The letters have been added to the quote for illustrative purposes.)

71. Lange also said that Norway's defense effort would continue, but he suggested certain conditions: "We must aim at rebuilding our defense without at the same time reducing the reconstruction program." Related to the question of external assistance, Lange noted the need for military supplies, the foreign currency dilemma, and the country's limited economic capacity. See *Ibid.*

72. *Ibid.*, pp. 26–27.

73. *Ibid.*, p. 30.

74. *Ibid.*, p. 28.

75. Soviet Ambassador Afanasiev delivered the note on January 29, and the Norwegians replied on February 1, 1949.

76. The text of the Soviet note can be found in *Norges Linje*, pp. 55–56. The question of bases had been raised several times, both in the U.S. and in Scandinavia. An influential figure in the Norwegian Labor movement, Karl Evang, cited in an extended commentary in an Oslo newspaper an article by Walter Lippmann in the January 21, 1949, *New York Herald Tribune*, which stated *inter alia* that the Atlantic Pact would be more than a mere association, for to Denmark and Norway it would mean deliveries of weapons and " . . . the development of Anglo-American sea and air installations in Scandinavia." Quoted by Evang in *Verdens Gang*, January 29, 1949.

77. Note cited in *Norges Linje*, pp. 57–58.

78. *Ibid.* (Italics added.) It should be noted that this formulation involved a warning as well as a reassurance to the U.S.S.R. regarding bases. The Norwegians thus established a conditional option.

79. On this point see Greve, *op. cit.*, p. 23.

80. In a lecture before the NATO Defense College a Norwegian stated the case as follows: The consideration of the Soviet Union was uppermost, but "One specific act had to be taken into consideration, namely the situation in Finland. It is our considered opinion that one should not exclude the possibility of Soviet countermeasures in Finland if Norway's position on the question of bases were to be changed. It will be easily understood that we do not have concrete information to rely on in this respect, but the Norwegian

government is of the opinion that it cannot be considered unlikely that the Soviet government might increase the number of Soviet armed forces on Finnish territory if the Norwegian base policy were to be changed." Skaug, *op. cit.*, p. 7.

81. For the text of the Soviet note delivered on February 5, 1949, see *Norges Linje*, pp. 59–61. It is interesting to note the quickness with which the Soviets picked up the conditional nature of the Norwegian commitment.

82. The Norwegian delegation, composed of Lange, Labor party parliamentary leader Oscar Torp, Dag Bryn of the Defense Ministry and a member of the Scandinavian Defense Commission, and Arne Gunneng of the Foreign Office, arrived in Washington on February 6, for a week. Their contact man in Washington was Charles E. "Chip" Bohlen who sat with them through most of their discussions with Congressional leaders, high State Department officials (including Secretary Acheson), and with President Truman. The Norwegians spent their days in Washington trying to win the Americans to the Norwegian position regarding the desirability of the establishment of defense staff arrangements with the United States as an alternative to direct membership in the Atlantic alliance, but, instead, the Americans persuaded the Norwegians that such an arrangement would not work for political reasons (particularly in Congress and in the National Security Council) and for legal reasons (the mandate of the mutual security acts).

On their return trip Lange and Torp stopped off in London for consultation with Foreign Secretary Bevin and other British leaders. These conversations took place on February 14 and generally confirmed that which had been discovered in the Washington talks (although it appeared to the Norwegians that the British were more favorably disposed to the concept of "informal arrangements" than were the Americans). Norway's Ambassador to the U.S. (Morgenstierne) and Ambassador to the U.K. (Prebensen) also participated in the talks. The delegation arrived back in Oslo on February 16, 1949. (These remarks are based on personal interviews with participants [in the spring of 1964 and the winter of 1967] and on Halvard Lange, *Norsk Utenrikspolitikk siden 1945*, p. 126.)

83. It is interesting to note that the Convention was not asked to take a position on the Atlantic Pact, which was not mentioned *per se*. Rather they were asked to support a resolution adopted by the National Committee of the Labor party by a vote of 34–4 on February 18 concluding that "Norway must solve its security problems in joint and binding collaboration in the sphere of defense policy with the Western Democracies." The debate, however, included many references to the Atlantic Pact. See *Protokoll*, p. 135.

84. *Ibid.*, pp. 120–21.

85. *Ibid.*, pp. 122–23.

86. *Ibid.*, p. 119.

87. *Ibid.* In this regard the Foreign Minister noted the experience of the Soviets during the Revolution, the civil war, the policies of the Western powers toward the U.S.S.R. during the interwar period, and Hitler's attack. Lange's unruffled view of the Soviets, however, was not echoed by the Defense Minister. Later in the debate, the Defense Minister not only reminded his listeners of the economic consequences of the decisions that were about to be made, but he said point blank: "First will I say that we must have the courage to recognize and express that we fear the expansionist foreign

policy of the Soviet Union, whatever the motive is. This fear is the primary motive in our foreign policy." (*Ibid.,* p. 158.) Lange spoke later, however, saying: "Let me say a few words on our evaluation of the risks in relation to the Soviet Union. The government sees it such that we do not think that the Soviet Union will purposely take the step, here or anyplace else in the world, with the *aim* of beginning a new war. Precisely because we do feel this way about the Soviets, we think that an explicit and formally anchored solidarity with the Western democracies will give us the greatest degree of security which is possible to attain in this imperfect world." (*Ibid.,* p. 187.) This somewhat contrary view of Soviet policy suggests that there was some tension within the government, but is probably best explained in terms of the multipronged strategy employed by the government in the effort to win an "in principle" endorsement of its foreign policy line by the National Convention. The arguments made by the different protagonists in the Labor Party Convention are beyond the scope of this study, but the spectrum ranged from those few who would have been quite willing to join in with the forces of anti-Bolshevism to those who were avowed pacifists and unabashed pro-Soviets. There were also the old-time neutralists, those who feared provoking the Russians, those who anticipated that the U.S. would retreat again into isolationism and leave the Europeans to deal alone with the Russians. The bugbear of April 9, 1940, was also raised (in the presence of former Foreign Minister Koht), and some asked how friends and enemies could be distinguished in such a dynamic and fluid political situation. Many were still bitter over the failure to come to terms with Sweden (and Prime Minister Erlander was called on to speak in an effort to placate the recalcitrants), and still others argued the ideological implications of the choice.

88. These (and the following) arguments are cited by Lange in *Ibid.,* pp. 120, 125, 131, 132.

89. *Ibid.* This form of argumentation clearly has its roots in the judgments made by the London government during the war when there were many discussions of a Scandinavian economic and military union. See *supra,* chap. ii.

90. *Ibid.,* p. 133.

91. *Ibid.,* p. 189.

92. This meeting came on February 24, six days after the National Convention. See *Stortingstidende,* "Redegj. fra utenriksministeren om forhandl. i Washington og London," February 24, 1949, pp. 288–93, debate pp. 293–335; reported in *Norges Linje,* pp. 36–45. The final draft of the Atlantic Pact was completed and published on March 18, 1949.

93. *Norges Linje,* p. 39.

94. *Ibid.,* p. 40. (Italics added.)

95. *Ibid.,* pp. 44–45.

96. The meeting was held on March 3, the vote was 118–11, and the following day Norwegian Ambassador Morgenstierne joined the discussions in Washington. The Storting also discussed the reply to the Soviet note of February 5, 1949. The focus of the discussion was on the proposals submitted by the Special Committee on Foreign Affairs, headed by Terje Wold. The Communists first submitted a proposal in effect to adjourn the meeting, but it was defeated. The proceedings of the secret session were released in 1964. See "Stortingets behandling av instilling fra Spesial Komiteén for saerlige utenriks-

politiske spørsmål og beredskaper angående utenriks-og sikkerhetspolitikken," (Innst. S. nr. 43 for 1949), *Stortings Dokument nr. 4.*

97. For the text of the Norwegian reply see *Norges Linje,* pp. 62–64. Fairly complete English translations of the four notes in the Soviet-Norwegian exchange can be found in Greve, *op. cit.,* pp. 28–31.

98. See *Stortingstidende,* "Utenriksministerens redegjørelse 24 februar," March 4, 1949, pp. 288–335.

99. March 22, 1949. On March 15, 1949, the Brussels Treaty Powers, Canada and the U.S. officially invited Norway (along with Denmark, Iceland, Italy, and Portugal) to accede to the Treaty.

100. See *Stortingstidende,* "Samtykke till ratifikasjon av Atlanter-havspakten," March 29, 1949, pp. 655–712. See Appendix B.

101. *Ibid.,* p. 712. The unreconstructed Laborites were Sverre Løberg and Carl Henry.

CHAPTER V

The Trend of
Norwegian Foreign Policy

The evolution of the Norwegian strategic image.—Prior to the outbreak of World War II, the authoritative Norwegian foreign policy elite perceived the structure of the international system in terms of great powers and small powers, with the process of international politics determined by the interactions among the great powers, whose respective aims, needs, and ambitions inevitably led to the condition of violent conflict. The Norwegian elite also assumed that small states were not similarly motivated and had no interests in the conflicts among the great powers. In addition it did not perceive Norway to be "strategically located" and further assumed that declarations of neutrality based on international law would be respected and effective in the event of a future great power conflict. The Norwegian goal therefore was to maintain freedom of action in order to keep out of war should it occur, and its policy was to create the conditions that would make neutrality possible. This meant, in peacetime, that Norway would have to avoid commitments to any powers that might become embroiled in a conflict in the foreseeable future, i.e., by definition, all great powers. Under these circumstances perceptions of friendship and hostility were not prominent in the policy articulations of Norwegian policy-makers, nor were questions of ideology since different criteria were employed to govern the selection of alternatives and consideration of contingencies.

It is clear that the key elements of the Norwegian strategic image were the perception of process (i.e., that the rules international law were, and would be, operational in any future war, thereby permitting neutrality) and their perception of their geographic location (i.e., that they were favorably endowed by a peripheral location vis-à-vis continental European struggles, a position that would enable them to remain aloof from any future European imbroglio).

April 9, 1940, proved these two key assumptions, on which Norwegian policy was based, to have been incorrect. The judgment of Norwegian policy-makers about the strategic importance of the western portion of Scandinavian peninsula was not shared by military authorities in Germany nor by political leaders in Britain (e.g., Churchill). And in the war which did ensue these strategic considerations outweighed Norway's unilateral declaration of neutrality that was undefended and without guarantee.

When the war did come, responsible policy-makers continued to assert the same judgments, arguing essentially that Norway was betrayed by an aggressive and hateful foreign great power. However, others made different evaluations, holding that the invasion of Norway was the result of its great strategic importance coupled with its isolationist policy that precluded effective aid in the event of attack, and an antipathy toward defense preparations that rendered impossible self-defense. This latter group soon gained control of the foreign policy-making machinery of the Norwegian government in London.

The strategic image of this new group was quite different from the former. This group perceived the system in terms of nation-states, some large and some small, but all states were a part of an inchoate and imperfect but nevertheless interdependent community in which it was difficult for one nation to isolate itself from the consequences of the actions of others. The process of international politics was seen as dominated by the great powers, and thus the substance of international politics would be determined for better or worse by the actions of and interactions among the great powers. Further the new elite judged the location of Norway to be "exposed" and "strategic" rather than peripheral; thus, Norway was thought to be particularly "involved" in international politics by virtue of her location.

As a result of these judgments a new action orientation emerged. No longer would Norway attempt to insure security by establishing in peacetime the conditions for neutrality in the event of war, but it would aim at collaborating with other nations to help insure that another war would not occur. It was no longer possible in the judgment of the new Norwegian policy elite to separate conditions of war from conditions of peace. Both were viewed as inescapable conditions of international life.

The policy that evolved from these new judgments was the "Atlantic policy," which looked to the solution of international problems and problems associated with national security on a regional basis. Later in the war, however, the Norwegian goal orientation was modified. Rather than work for the solution of national security problems on the basis of *regional* co-operation, the establishment of the United Nations Organization meant that the dilemma of national security was to be solved on the basis of *universal* collaboration.

This new goal orientation resulted in another change in Norwegian foreign policy that manifested itself in two phases. The first phase might be described as the "United Nations policy," the aim of which was to establish the prerequisites for an effective solution of national security problems on a universal basis through collective security. This policy therefore supported the establishment of a "strong" universal international organization in which those who possessed power would be given the authority to use it. This first phase of Norwegian foreign policy was successful in the sense that a "strong" international organization with security functions was in fact established. Norwegian goal orientation was then refocused, aiming at the creation of the necessary conditions for the successful functioning of the United Nations Organization. This led to a new policy, one that has been referred to as the policy of "bridgebuilding," that is a behavioral pattern characterized by taking all actions that would facilitate congenial relations among the great powers and refraining from all actions that might affect adversely the relations among the great powers. During this period Norwegian security policy was rooted in the UN as a security instrument and therefore depended on the ability of the Security Council to meet threats to the peace effectively.

Consequently, one of the crucial variables underlying the Norwegian policy of bridgebuilding was the ability of the great powers to co-operate in reaching the solution of those problems that could threaten the existence of peace. In early 1948, however, the Norwegians acknowledged the existence of tensions in international politics that undermined the basic assumptions of the United Nations as a security instrument. Finally the Norwegians perceived a threat to world peace (the existence of military and political vacuums in strategically located areas during times of rising tensions) that required them to search for means other than the United Nations and universal collaboration as the basis of their security policy.

Two dimensions of the Norwegian strategic image now became significant in the consideration of the alternative for an effective and adequate security policy. One concerned a conviction about the process of international politics (referred to as "historical experience") that in times of conflict powerful protagonists will pre-empt areas of strategic importance. And second, the judgment that postwar bloc configurations and the new "techniques" of warfare had made Norway an area of strategic importance. After the Norwegians perceived the existence of deep-rooted conflict among the two great powers, the two judgments converged, leading to the important conclusions that (1) Norwegian national security was threatened, and, moreover, (2) a weak Norway was itself a threat to international stability.

As a result, the goal orientation of the Norwegian government was again modified. It looked primarily to the establishment of a "new equilibrium" that would again provide the basis for international stability, and secondarily to an increase in the defense capability of Norway. Operationalizing the primary goal suggested to the policy elite Norwegian ties to a broad-based regional arrangement that would possess political, economic, and military viability and vitality. Moreover, the realization of the secondary goal was not feasible, for a variety of reasons,[1] in the absence of Norwegian collaboration with other nations. Thus, in order to make both goals operational, the Norwegians opted for a traditional strategy: participation in an alliance system. The Norwegian foreign policy elite was again probing for a regional solution to its security dilemma.

Norwegian consideration of a Scandinavian alternative.— Although the Norwegian government had, during the period of the war, rejected the concept of a neutral Scandinavian bloc, and even though it was clear that a neutral Scandinavian bloc was not consistent either with the Norwegians' perception of the dangers that inhered in international politics or with their view of the best strategy to re-create international stability and a working foundation for the UN, the first attempt to shape a regional solution for Norwegian security problems was made within the Scandinavian area.

Barring a radical revision of the basic assumptions held by both the Swedish and Norwegian foreign policy elites, it was predictable that the attempt to create a Scandinavian alliance would not succeed. In order to examine the problems encountered in the Scandinavian defense negotiations, a comparative examination of the strategic images held by each of the major actors should be reviewed.

First, both the Norwegians and the Swedes envisioned their national purpose in terms of the maintenance of independence and the freedom to shape their own internal affairs. The geographic dimension of the cognitive component of the strategic image of both was similar; they both conceived themselves as occupying a strategically important area. However, their respective images of process resulted in a fundamentally different evaluation of the consequences for each of them of their exposed position. The Swedes tended to view their location in terms of its meaning for potentially interested great powers. They reasoned that if the Scandinavian peninsula were of strategic importance, it would be so for both sides, and thus all, in the absence of provocation, would have an incentive to leave the area in peace. The Norwegians, on the other hand, seemed to view the threat to their own security and to Scandinavia in terms of a "threat situation" rather than in terms of a potential threat from one or another side in a future conflict. The Norwegians reasoned that in times of tension it was very destabilizing and therefore dangerous to have strategically important areas inadequately defended, a situation they viewed as dangerous and tension-producing because, even without provocation, it tempted pre-emption by strategy-conscious great powers. Such pre-emption did not necessarily require an aggressive great power, for it might be carried out for defensive reasons. Nevertheless, when it did occur, the result would be the same for the Norwegian people, and thus the only way to prevent such an "unpremeditated explosion" (as the Foreign Minister referred to the danger) was to insure in advance that pre-emptive occupation would not be feasible. The result of these different views however can be simply stated: the Swedes calculated highly the probability that they could keep outside a future conflict if it should occur; [2] the Norwegians conversely attached a very low probability to their opportunity to escape involvement in the event of a future conflict.

Their respective images of process also included another dimension which affected their policy judgments. The Swedes seemed to judge that the building of great power blocs was in and of itself destabilizing behavior; thus their offer of an isolated Scandinavian alliance to the Norwegians and the Danes served two purposes: first, it would tend to limit the comprehensiveness of the evolving Western bloc system, and second, it would preclude a provocative great power foothold in the Scandinavian area. Both of these aims, had they become accomplished facts, would have served what the Swedes viewed as in the best interests of national security *and* international stability. The Norwegians, on the other hand, tended to view the process of international politics in a more complex way. They felt that international stability was a *sine qua non* for national security, that the two were inseparable and could best be guaranteed on a universal basis. Once it was clear that a universal collective security system did not exist, the Norwegians felt that regional security systems would best serve the stability of international political relations by creating a "new equilibrium" that would, in turn, serve as the foundation for mutual respect among the great powers. The Norwegians were clearly more "system oriented" than were the Swedes, and it is obvious that they viewed their national fate as irrevocably tied to the course of events in international politics.[3] Thus the Norwegians looked to the creation of new "power factors" in the world, for in their view it was weakness leading to miscalculation, and ambiguity leading to misinformation, that would most likely be responsible for a new war.

In short the Norwegians did not adhere to the Swedish concept of the "divisibility of peace"; in the judgment of the Norwegians, if war came, Norway was certain to be involved. The primary Norwegian concern therefore was to create a "power factor" sufficiently strong to deter pre-emption and to prevent miscalculation and misinformation, and thereby the unwanted war.

Thus the temptation to argue that Norway was more concerned with short-term military security in the event of war while the Swedes were concerned with employing political means to help insure that the unwanted war did not occur is to be avoided as beside the point.[4] It is true that the Swedes did not share the anxiety apparently felt by the Norwegians in the situation in which they both found themselves in 1948–49. Thus the Swedes were hoping for a solution to Norway's security dilemma that would not, *in the view of the Swedes*, exacerbate tensions. However, because the Norwegian view of both the existing dangers and of the optimal basis for stability and tension reduction differed fundamentally with those same judgments of the Swedes, the Norwegians found themselves in the position of being able to reconcile the requirements of their short-term security needs with their long-term aim of contributing to the evolution of more stable international relationships.

Thus the different strategic images of the Norwegians and the Swedes resulted in different operational goal orientations that, in turn, required different strategies. With regard to their respective goals, the Norwegians were oriented toward alliances as a means of strengthening their own national security and international stability. The underlying assumption of the policy was the judgment that politico-military vacuums were destabilizing to international security and a threat to national security. The Swedes were oriented toward the maintenance of conditions that would permit neutrality in war. Thus the policy of "nonalliance" was modified in favor of Norway and Denmark in the hope of precluding their membership in the Western alliance system. The underlying assumption was that Scandinavia as a strategic unit need not be involved in a future conflict, and the specific assumptions were (1) a great power foothold on the Scandinavian peninsula would be provocative, making the Swedish position more vulnerable, and (2) politico-military blocs were destabilizing. The Norwegians and the Swedes thus disagreed both on the optimal strategy to deter war and the optimal strategy to guarantee national security, and it was because of these fundamentally different evaluations that the Scandinavian defense alliance was not formed.

If the absence of similar evaluations of the "facts" of their respective security problems and their resulting inability to agree on the optimal strategy to solve these problems was the cause of the failure of Scandinavian defense negotiations to reach a positive result, then some examination of their commencement is required, especially since some have speculated on the purpose of the Norwegians' entering the negotiations in the first place.

As the title of the preceding chapter implies, the range of alternatives, as far as the Norwegians were concerned, was not a Scandinavian bloc *or* an Atlantic bloc, but rather an alternative on the one side of a Scandinavian bloc *related* in some way to the Atlantic powers, or membership in the Atlantic arrangement directly. It is to be recalled that the Norwegians agreed to the investigation of the Scandinavian Defense Commission on the basis of the political assumptions embraced by the Swedes, i.e., that the investigation would proceed *as if* the proposed Scandinavian alliance were to be neutral. Thus, the technical findings of the Scandinavian defense investigations might have resulted in a revision of the assumptions of the Norwegians and therefore have made possible the establishment of a Scandinavian defense alliance. The fact however, is that the findings of the defense investigation tended rather to reinforce the assumptions of the Norwegians; thus it must be assumed that only the above-mentioned options envisioned by the Norwegians were the operational alternatives during the period of the *political* discussions. This conclusion is further supported by the Norwegian Foreign Minister's many statements prior to, during, and after the political discussions in January, 1949, and it is this point which seems to have been missed in subsequent analyses of this watershed period in the foreign policies of the Scandinavian countries.

The subtle argumentation in which Lange engaged regarding the question of "an isolated Scandinavian pact without formal ties to the West" has already been pointed out. The continued repetition of this argument reveals, in context, that Lange was placing emphasis on the word *formal,* while the Swedes were emphasizing (without equivocation) the word *isolated,* i.e., the absence of ties with any great powers. In a statement to the Storting in February, 1949, Lange stated fairly clearly what it was the Norwegians were advocating during the period of the political discussions. He said that the two sides were not in agreement on the "character of the alliance-free pact" and that the central question concerned the nature such a pact would assume in the absence of a connection to the evolving Western alliance system. Perhaps even more revealing, however, is the Foreign Minister's statement that

From the Norwegian side, in order to reach a common solution, we were willing to consider giving up the idea of a formal connection to the more comprehensive security system which is evolving in order to reach a common [Scandinavian] solution.[5]

The Foreign Minister pointed out that this would have involved a substantial concession from the Norwegian side, but the concession was never made because

In the meantime we found that we were not able to accept that we should not discuss politico-security realities with the Western great powers.[6]

Thus the essential political difference is revealed in bold relief. The Norwegians were willing to make the concession that there would be no *formal* ties between a "neutral" Scandinavian bloc and the West, but that "understandings" and contacts would nevertheless have to exist between the two entities.[7] The Swedes could not accept this orientation. As Lange himself stated in this same address, the Swedes persisted in their view "that the proposed defense pact must in all respects, both formally and in reality, be isolated." Lange said that the Norwegians, on the other hand, did not feel justified in precluding for themselves the possibilities of discussing security problems with the West.

The Norwegians viewed the proposed Scandinavian bloc as ostensibly "alliance-free" but nevertheless loosely and informally tied to the Western bloc. The Swedes (*never* giving evidence to the contrary) could not accept this concept of a Scandinavian subsystem within a larger Western security system. In fact, as early as May, 1948, the Swedish Foreign Minister noted that among the advocates of Scandinavian co-operation are those interested in Scandinavian inclusion in a Western bloc. He added, "It is clear that the Swedish Government, which does not wish to join a West bloc, is no less unwilling to do so *via* a Scandinavian alliance."

The Swedish position was unequivocal, and it is quite obvious that what the Norwegians advocated, if accepted, would have fundamentally altered the political basis of Swedish foreign policy. Lange's reference, however, to the investigations of the Scandinavian Defense Commission as supporting the Norwegian view is indicative of Lange's strategy: he was perhaps hopeful of altering Swedish assumptions when the Swedes viewed their implications in the light of the technical findings. The problem was, however, that for the Swedes the question of the political basis of their foreign policy was not susceptible of empirical argument. It was based on a principle that had stood the test of time, that was rooted in a strategic image that did not admit to the existence of the same "facts" as did the Norwegians' evaluation of the situation in international politics.

Thus, more specifically, the Scandinavian defense negotiations failed because the Norwegians desired a Scandinavian bloc as in fact, if not organically, a subsystem within a larger Western security arrangement, and this desire was the issue between Norway and Sweden that became the substance of the political negotiations. Thus, to answer the question posed above, the implication is that the Norwegians entered the political discussions because the political issue between the two might have been resolved in favor of Norway, especially in view of the findings of the technical investigations.

Although no attempt has been made here to examine systematically the *internal* dynamics of the Norwegian foreign policy process, it is worth mentioning that the Scandinavian defense negotiations probably did work to political advantage of the authoritative foreign policy elite on the domestic scene. Although the point about to be made is usually advanced in the polemical literature, suggesting a "charade" on the part of Lange, it does have to its credit the recognition that the prerequisites for a Scandinavian alliance never did exist.

The "charade hypothesis" in its basic form, is somewhat diabolical, suggesting that the government engaged in the exercise of the Scandinavian defense negotiations in order to overcome domestic political opposition to Norwegian participation in a Western alliance system; thus the Foreign Minister was never "serious" about the Scandinavian discussions. The prototype argument would be as follows:

Within Norway a hardcore element existed that was opposed to alliances. This hardcore included a small group on the right that would have Norway follow an independent national policy based on the traditional principles of neutrality, and left-wing members of the Labor party who were opposed to Norwegian association in a Western bloc for ideological and political reasons. Some among this latter group, in fact, were decidedly cool toward the Marshall Plan for the same reason. Thus if Lange were to solve what he perceived as the Norwegian security dilemma, he had to win over one or both of these groups. Thus in early 1948, when Lange began to recognize publicly the existence of international tensions that undermined the effectiveness of the UN, he succeeded in turning attention to a co-operative Scandinavian effort to solve Norwegian security problems. By so doing he won an important preliminary victory, for the neutralists and pacifists in his own party were induced, by accepting the concept of a Scandinavian alliance, to accept the underlying assumption that Norway could not provide national security unilaterally. Thus the "pacifists/neutralists" became "Scandinavians." However, once it was demonstrated that the Scandinavian alliance could not provide the security that was required, the "new" Scandinavians had unwittingly sloughed the only possible basis for effective opposition to Norwegian association with the Western bloc and were left with little choice except to accept the Atlantic Pact. Thus once the neutralists had been converted to Scandinavians, the domestic political battle had been largely won.

Although the analysis of the negotiations provided above suggests that this imputation of motive is probably without foundation, even a superficial examination of the political problems faced by the government indicates the utility of the Scandinavian defense negotiations (and especially the findings of the joint investigations) in overcoming the domestic political obstacles that had to be surmounted if any multilateral security policy were to be pursued.

Indeed, when the final discussions of the Atlantic pact occurred in the Storting, the opposition's arguments were weak, inconsistent, and doctrinal.[8] The debate, for the most part took place between the Communists and the Laborites,[9] and the spokesmen for the government gave innocuous answers to largely irrelevant objections. Certainly the potential thrust of the opposition, logically and politically undermined by their initial acceptance of a Scandinavian solution, was further deflected by the extended period of the Scandinavian investigations, an alternative that was never really *debated* in the Storting until *after* it was no longer an alternative. A simultaneous rather than sequential consideration of the two alternatives would have certainly affected the internal fight in the Labor party. Furthermore, the Lange-Torp mission to Washington delayed even further extended debate of the Atlantic alternative, which by the time of decision in early March was the only remaining multilateral security option open to the Norwegians. Thus, when the conclusion was drawn that a neutral Scandinavia could not be self-sufficient either in defense preparations or in the event of war, and once it was clear that the Swedes would not accept the concept of *informal* ties between Scandinavia and the West in the area of security policy, the neutralists-turned-Scandinavians were inextricably caught in an inexorable logic that permitted them no other course than to accept, as most of them did, the only other alternative, in addition to the non-aggression pact with the U.S.S.R., open at the time: Norwegian membership in the Atlantic Alliance.

However, while the internal political process mentioned briefly here raises interesting questions related to parliamentary control over foreign policy and to the tactical genius of political leadership, the evidence seems to show clearly that the basic "charade" assumption is not tenable and is certainly not consistent with the decisive issues in the negotiations.

It is sufficient to say that the government probably benefited from the "public education" gained as a result of the attempted Scandinavian solution to the problem of Norwegian security.

Another proffered and more widely accepted explanation for the failure of the Scandinavian defense negotiations and Norway's subsequent membership in the Atlantic alliance is that which suggests American pressure in general, and specifically the refusal of the U.S. to give arms supply priority to a Scandinavian bloc as the "cause" of the breakdown.

As acknowledged above, the report of the Scandinavian Defense Commission stated that substantial rearmament would have to be undertaken in Norway and Denmark, and Sweden would have to engage in a fairly comprehensive program of arms modernization. This immediately raised the question of arms supplies, for it was certain that neither Norway nor Denmark, neither of whom possessed significant armaments industries, could rearm on a substantial scale without undermining their international financial position and ultimately their reconstruction programs, and Sweden acknowledged her lack of capacity to provide the necessary arms to her neighbors. Thus Norway and Denmark would be required to procure arms from abroad.

As previously mentioned, all of the actors in the negotiations were agreed on this question of arms procurement necessitated by the requirement to increase their defense capability. One intervening factor, however, somewhat complicates the consideration of the question of the relation of American arms deliveries to the eventual failure of the negotiations. A State Department Press Officer,[10] one week prior to the second round of negotiations in Copenhagen, announced concerning American arms supplies that "It is natural that such supplies as may be available should go to countries associated with us in collective defense arrangements."[11] Although it is not absolutely clear whether the statement was directed specifically toward Scandinavia, it nevertheless caused some consternation in the North, as it did in the U.S. The statement was labeled as "poorly timed" and "careless" by many, and James Reston, writing in the *New York Times* suggested that it was intended to test the aims of several of the European countries with regard to the proposed Atlantic Pact. Reston indicated that the United States was hopeful of gaining the co-operation of Denmark (and Greenland), Portugal (and the Azores), and Iceland, Eire, Norway, and Sweden, "all of whom have certain facilities necessary to an effective Atlantic security system."[12]

Undoubtedly, there was great interest in the U.S. regarding Scandinavian participation in the Atlantic defense system under negotiation, but Reston, again writing in the *New York Times* after the failure of the Scandinavian defense negotiations, questioned the wisdom of the U.S. policy toward the Scandinavian discussions.[13]

Reston discussed the Atlantic Pact as embodying two primary concepts: the political and the military. He indicated pressure, asserting that the questions of Scandinavia's membership in the alliance was discussed by the National Security Council in the U.S., and N.S.C. analysts had concluded that "the North Atlantic Pact would definitely be weakened, in strategic and psychological terms, if Norway and Denmark did not join. . . . " Reston suggests, however, that the National Security Council may have overemphasized the military concept of the Pact at the expense of the political value to both Scandinavia and the North Atlantic Alliance of a neutral Scandinavian bloc. Further, he suggests that military concepts had dictated the American position regarding the Scandinavian defense negotiations in general and defense supplies in particular. The problematical point that emerges, however, is the assumption made by Reston and by many others [14] examining the same issues, that in some way the U.S. might have been able to alter the outcome of the Scandinavian defense negotiations by having taken a different position with regard to the question of the deliveries of defense material to a neutral Scandinavian bloc.[15] Although this argument has appeal, it fails to take account of the deep political schism that existed between Norway and Sweden regarding the relationship of the proposed Scandinavian pact to the larger Western security system.

Speaking hypothetically, for illustration, it can be said that *if* the Oslo meeting had been successful, that is, if Sweden had submitted to the Norwegian demand to have consultations with the leaders of the Western alliance system regarding what the Norwegian Foreign Minister referred to as "politico-security realities," then (but only then) would the "prerequisites" for a Scandinavian alliance have existed from the point of view of Norway. And, were this concession made by Sweden, and had the U.S. persisted in its policy of arms deliveries to non-associated states, then it could be assumed that the U.S. had in fact blitzed the Scandinavian defense negotiations. Although it might be argued that the U.S. would not have changed its articulated policy, this hypothetical confrontation did not in fact take place, since the necessary prerequisites (i.e., *political* agreement between Norway and Sweden) for the confrontation between the U.S. and the Scandinavians failed to materialize.

Consequently, with regard to the arms supply hypothesis the conclusion must be reached that *the question of military supplies was not decisive in the Scandinavian defense negotiations* due to the inability of the participants to agree on the larger question of the political orientation of the proposed alliance, an issue that had plagued the discussion of a "Scandinavian solution" since the spring of 1948.[16]

Finally, a related (and very common) explanation for the choice made by the Norwegian government to join the Atlantic alliance suggests that economic implications were decisive, that Norwegian Socialists were not about to sacrifice their social and economic programs for defense. This analysis is obviously credible and was on several occasions explicitly supported by one of the principal Norwegian actors, the Defense Minister, who argued that in the absence of external aid either (1) the time period for reconstruction would have to be extended or (2) the security program would have to be reduced.

It can be assumed straight away that both of these conditions of a self-reliant security policy were unacceptable to the Norwegians. The government had never considered reducing the defense effort; in fact, quite the contrary is the case as is demonstrated by the extraordinary defense appropriations in 1948. The second condition, postponing the recovery program, was undoubtedly distasteful for many obvious reasons, not the least of which is that the Labor party was enjoying its first absolute parliamentary majority and was to face elections again in the fall of 1949.

The examination of the evolution of Norwegian security policy provided herein does not permit a definitive statement of the role played by economic considerations in the final choice that was made by the government. However, the examination that has been made does demonstrate that economic considerations were not *initially* involved, for the search for regional security arrangements began essentially as a step toward the stabilization of international political relations as a means toward increasing the security of Norway. Thus economic considerations supported but were not essential to the choice that was made, and they were collateral rather than central in the development of alternatives by the Norwegian government, since the definition of alternatives tended to be based on politico-strategic rather than economic criteria.

Conclusion.—In short, the failure of the Scandinavian defense negotiations and the subsequent decision to join the North Atlantic Alliance can be explained by reference to, and was consistent with, the Norwegian strategic image as it had evolved by the end of the summer of 1948. It may well be that the most desirable solution from the Norwegian point of view would have been a semi-independent Scandinavian bloc loosely tied to a Western alliance that would have guaranteed the Northern bloc's security in the event of war. Such an arrangement would have satisfied the deterrence goal as well as the national security goal of the Norwegian government; in addition it would have involved the least provocation (in the Norwegian view of the possible alternatives) to the Soviet Union. The inability of the Swedes and the Norwegians to agree on such an arrangement left the Norwegians with no acceptable choice other than the Atlantic Alliance, for the failure to join the Alliance would have required the denial of every political and strategic judgment made by the Norwegian foreign policy elite over the preceding nine years, and particularly the preceding twelve months, and would have required the Labor party to discredit its own Foreign Minister. Thus to the extent that the other authoritative decision-makers shared the environmental judgments of the Foreign Minister, the decision to join the Atlantic Alliance was certain to be made, and could have been avoided only by a major denunciation of the existing political leadership or by an intervening environmental event that would have been perceived in such a way so as to result in a substantial restructuring of the Norwegian strategic image.

Consequently, the Labor party conference could have altered the outcome only by forcing a thorough purge of its own leadership. Although both institutional mechanisms and traditions favored the continued incumbency of the Norwegian government—and therefore their preferred values and outcomes, many of the national and international moves that have been reviewed are probably best understood in the context of the leadership maintenance function of the Norwegian elite on the domestic scene.

This interesting problem, however, is the subject of another study. The crucial finding for this *ex post facto* analysis is that images and outcomes corresponded very closely, and potential mediating factors were not sufficiently powerful to alter the outcome. Examining only elite images would have left unexplained certain of the tactical domestic and diplomatic maneuvers that were reviewed above, but the final outcome, given the alternatives, was predictable from the image structure itself. There is no reason to believe that the needs for foreign policy leaders to reduce dissonance are any less than those of the rest of us. Thus, if the image structure and content can be correctly defined, the range of relevant choices available to decision makers can be reduced considerably. In short, given a certain range of alternatives, knowledge of the decision-makers strategic image permits the projection of probable outcomes.

Obviously, intervening factors might alter the predicted outcomes. As mentioned above in this case, the substitution of authoritative decision-makers for those whose images were examined might have (indeed probably would have) altered the outcome. However, there were also observable forces working against the probability of such a substitution's occurring. Thus, for future study, it would be important to examine both the relation between modifications in the structure and content of elite images with changes in elites and to study the stability (or "staying power") of decisional units during periods of crisis or, at a lower level, during periods when cardinal choices are consciously under consideration—as was the situation in the case presented here.

It is normally assumed that feedback processes may operate so as to modify images, but it is also known that images are remarkably resilient and that individuals protect themselves from dissonance when image and "reality" do not correspond. The many references to "historical experience" by Lie and Lange would seem to demonstrate the operation of a feedback modification process, but as Chapter II points out, modification of authoritative images was effected only after a change of top personnel in the foreign office. The former leadership (Koht's entourage) maintained their previous views and "explained away" or otherwise ignored non-corresponding and non-reinforcing events. Moreover, the many subsequent references to "historical experience" by the new leadership over the nine-year period examined seemed to be image-confirming rather than image-modifying. In short, it appears not to have been a catastrophic historical event that modified images; rather, it was a catastrophic historical event that "confirmed" the image articulated by non-authoritative "outs" and discredited the images of the authoritative decision-makers, legitimating, thereby, the views of the former dissidents and their claims for authority. Thus, for future study it will be important to specify the conditions under which the images of authoritative elites are significantly modified by either a catastrophic experience or image-denying information over a slice of time or by changes in elite personnel. However, dissonance theory, the ability of some elites to take actions that are self-fulfilling, and the "lesson" of this case would all tend to favor the hypothesis that *authoritative strategic images are substantially modified primarily by substitutions of authoritative decision-makers.* If this hypothesis can be confirmed by other studies, the prospect for achieving widely corresponding images among international elites is dim indeed, especially since socialization and recruitment patterns of decision-makers suggest the superordinate hypothesis that substitutions of incumbents in stable polities will normally not result in substitutions of authoritative elite images. Consequently, we are left with the gloomy conclusion that strategic images, and therefore foreign policy outcomes, are radically modified primarily as a result of either (1) a political disaster accompanied by elite turnover—as in this study or (2) revolution; that is, in both cases the replacement of authoritative decision-makers by those with different socialization experience and recruitment patterns.

Consequently, the job for the policy scientist is suggested. If revolution and political disaster are thought to be too costly, but if image modification is thought to be essential, then new techniques and strategies for achieving corresponding (i.e., identical or complementary) images among national decision-making elites must be explored.

1. The articulations of the foreign policy elite reveal two classes of reasons. Some were objective: Norway's limited economic resources and capacity; others were subjective: a prior commitment to the reestablishment of Norwegian living standards.

2. Östen Undén the Swedish Foreign Minister at the time of the Scandinavian Defense negotiations, stated very clearly the nature of the Swedish judgment in this regard in 1957. He said that in the event of a strategic nuclear war between the U.S. and the U.S.S.R. it was absurd to think that Sweden could affect the outcome, and as long as Sweden was not involved in any bloc it was "difficult to think of any motive for an attack on Sweden during the short and violent duel with which such a war would begin and probably end. Assume on the other hand that the nuclear weapons are put in mothballs. . . . It would then be a matter of conventional arms. How would this affect Sweden's position? Well, this is practically the same type of attack we were thinking of after the Second World War when we decided not to enter any great power bloc. The two bombs dropped on Japan had then not really come into the picture . . . we have no reason willingly to join an alliance group if war has the character, militarily speaking, that the Second World War had. We can therefore start from the assumption that in both these cases of general warfare there are very powerful reasons why Sweden should try to pursue a policy of neutrality. . . ."—Speech by the Foreign Minister at the Conference of the Social Democratic Youth Federation, November 5, 1957 (Stockholm: Royal Ministry of Foreign Affairs), mimeograph.

3. At the time of the defense negotiations the Swedes were clearly more "regionally oriented" in terms of what they perceived as the balance of power in the North and especially the "situation of Finland," which was viewed as contingent on Swedish abstention from a close military relationship with the West. See Gunnar Heckscher, *Sweden and the East-West Conflict* (Stockholm: The Swedish Institute, 1961), p. 4; Herbert Tingsten, "Issues in Swedish Foreign Policy," *Foreign Affairs*, XXXVII (April, 1959), 479; and Samuel Abrahamsen, *Sweden's Foreign Policy* (Washington, D.C.: Public Affairs Press, 1957).

4. Ironically, a variation of this argument, employing the same assumptions, is made by one of Norway's leading foreign policy analysts. Nils Ørvik, *The Decline of Neutrality 1914–1941* (Oslo: Tanum, 1953), p. 267, writes, regarding Norway's subsequent membership in NATO and Sweden's continued policy of freedom from alliances, that "Norway is likely to be better off if an unprovoked Russian attack is inevitable and will come within a few years, while Sweden will profit from a long period of peace."

5. Reference here is to Lange's statement in the Storting on February 3, 1949, reported in Utenriksdepartementets Pressetjeneste, *Norges Linje* (Oslo: Tiden, 1949), pp. 29–30.

6. *Ibid.*

7. The point made here represents undoubtedly one of the greater ironies of the postwar period. The U.S.S.R. opposed the Swedes' concept of a neutral Scandinavian alliance because they thought it would become a part of the Western alliance system, while this was precisely the concept which the Swedes were resisting. The Americans on the other hand initially refused priority on military supplies to a "neutral" Scandinavian alliance, which had it in fact come into existence, would hardly have been neutral. The final irony is the Soviet protest in late January of a Scandinavian alliance, which they disliked least, just prior to its failure, leading to Norwegian and Danish participation in the wider security arrangement which the Soviets opposed the most.

8. See Torolf Elster, "Norges utenrikspolitiske stilling," *Økonomi og Politik,* XXV (1951), 39.

9. See *Infra,* Appendix B.

10. The statement was made on January 14, 1949, by Michael J. McDermott.

11. See James Reston, *New York Times,* January 15, 1949.

12. *Ibid.*

13. Reference here is to two articles by James Reston in the *New York Times,* February 11, 1949 and February 20, 1949.

14. Compare for example, Raymond Lindgren, *Norway-Sweden: Union, Disunion, and Scandinavian Integration* (Princeton: Princeton University Press, 1959), pp. 261–66; Franklin D. Scott, *The United States and Scandinavia* (Cambridge: Harvard University Press, 1950), p. 307. The U.S. later denied that priorities had been established on arms supplies.

15. This is not to suggest that the Americans did not "think" they were influencing the outcome of the Scandinavian defense negotiations, for there is no reason to believe that the U.S. had a perfect information regarding the ongoing discussions. It is quite plausible that the State Department *thought* it was influencing the outcome of the talks as a result of its statement on arms supplies, when in fact it was not.

16. This discussion of the American position vis-à-vis the Scandinavian countries is not intended to suggest that the Scandinavians were not under considerable pressure. Indeed they were being pressured by the U.S., the British, and the Soviet Union all during this period. The Soviets from 1947 opposed all concepts of any kind of a Scandinavian defense arrangement, arguing that it would be little more than a link in the American security system, and when the Scandinavian Defense Commission was established the domestic Communists in Scandinavia were "markedly hostile to the idea." See Tim Greve, *Norway and NATO* (Oslo: Oslo University Press, 1959), p. 10, and Halvard Lange, *Norsk Utenrikspolitikk siden 1945* (Oslo: Tanum, 1952), p. 97. The British had reportedly warned the Swedes about leading Scandinavia "down the blind road of neutrality," and the Americans obviously were looking for as wide a formal participation in the Atlantic Alliance as possible. From the point of view of world politics in an era of intercontinental

bombers (as in the decade following the war), and in view of the so-called polar strategy which had emerged in the U.S. it can hardly be doubted that the U.S. desired Scandinavian participation, or at least the participation of Norway and Denmark with their strategically important overseas possessions of Greenland and Svalbard (even though the latter archipelago could not be fortified).

APPENDIX A

Composition of Parliament after the Elections of 1936-1965*

Party	1936	1945	1949	1953	1957	1961	1965
Communist		11	...	3	1	...	...
Labor	70	76	85	77	78	74	68
Socialist People's ...						2	2
Liberal	23	20	21	15	15	14	18
Center	18	10	12	14	15	16	18
Christian People's ..	2	8	9	14	12	15	13
Conservative	26	25	23	27	29	29	31

* Olaf Chr. Torp, *Stortinget* (Olso: Johan Grundt Tanum, 1962), p. 14; and Vilhelm Haffner, *Stortinget* (Olso: Johan Grundt Tanum, 1946), p. 110; *News of Norway,* September 16, 1965, p. 109.

Data on the Debate regarding the Ratification of the Atlantic Pact*

PARTY	PARLIAMEN-TARY REPRE-SENTATION	SPEAKERS	SPEECHES	CC †	PER CENT OF CC
Labor 76	13	14§	950.0	40.8
Communist 11	6	8‖	698.5	30.0
Liberal 20	7	7	370.0	16.0
Conservative 25	2‡	2	181.5	7.8
Christian People's .. 8	2‡	2	98.0	4.2
Farmer's 10	1‡	1	31.0	1.2
Total 150	31	34	2,329.0	100.0

* See *Stortingstidende*, "Samtykke til ratifikasjon av Atlanterhavspakten," March 29, 1949, pp. 657–712.

† "Column centimeters" of "relevant" debate. Not included: introductory remarks by the presiding officer, a discussion of opening the galleries to the public, and voting procedures and reports.

‡ Represents a statement of position by the party's parliamentary leader and/or assistant leader.

§ Foreign Minister Lange spoke twice.

‖ Stortingsmenn Vogt and Løvlien each spoke twice.

Bibliographic Note

In addition to the English language citations included in the footnotes, the English-speaking student with interests in Norwegian politics (including, of course, Norwegian foreign policy) should consult three relatively recent and important studies of Norway. As an introduction, JAMES A. STORING's *Norwegian Democracy* (Oslo: Universitetsforlaget, 1963) is a very readable and reliable account of the primary structures of Norwegian national and local government cast in a conventional "comparative" politics format. A stimulating and provocative analysis of the functioning Norwegian political system is provided in HARRY ECKSTEIN's *Division and Cohesion in Democracy: A Study of Norway* (Princeton: Princeton University Press, 1966), where he presents an analysis of the Norwegian political system in terms of his previously published monograph, "A Theory of Stable Democracy" (Research Monograph Number 10 by the Center of International Studies, Princeton University, 1961). Finally, the student interested in Norway or in comparative parties or electoral behavior should consult HENRY VALEN and DANIEL KATZ, *Political Parties in Norway: A Community Study* (Oslo: Universitetsforlaget, 1964), for a penetrating analysis (based on survey methods and contrasted with the American party system) of the structure and functioning of political parties in the Norwegian political system with special emphasis on decision-making and on oligarchic tendencies.

In addition to the landmark studies noted above, other important sources in English include *The Norway Yearbook*, published annually by Johan Grundt Tanum Forlag in Oslo, which provides a wide variety of background information on Norwegian political, social, and economic life. *The Times* (London) carried accounts of the Norwegian government in exile during the Second World War, and the political events of the postwar years are well-summarized in *Norway Digest* (1946–48) and *News of Norway* (1948–present), both published in English by the Norwegian Information Office in Washington, D.C. The latter, particularly, provides a high quality weekly synopsis of Norwegian political developments. Those interested in Norwegian and Scandinavian politics are also referred to *The American Scandinavian Review*, published by the American Scandinavian Foundation. The *Review* carries periodic lead articles on the foreign policies of the five Nordic countries and each issue summarizes political events of the past quarter year in each of the Nordic countries. Also helpful is *The Norseman* (1943–1958), which provided by far the most varied publication on internal and external affairs of the Nordic countries during the fifteen years of its existence.

Index

Index